HOMEGROWN DEFENSE
biofuels & national security

HOMEGROWN DEFENSE
biofuels & national security

FRANK J. GAFFNEY, JR.

GAL LUFT

ROBERT ZUBRIN

WESLEY K. CLARK

BURL HAIGWOOD

GREG DOLAN

FRANK J. GAFFNEY, JR.
Publisher

BEN LERNER
Editor-in-Chief

DAVID REABOI
Associate Editor

sec[u]refreedom.org

PRINTED IN THE UNITED STATES OF AMERICA

ISBN 978-0-9822947-4-1

1 2 3 4 5 6 7 8 9 10

FIRST EDITION

THE CENTER FOR SECURITY POLICY
1901 Pennsylvania Avenue, Suite 201
Washington, DC 20006
Phone: (202) 835-9077
Email: info@securefreedom.org

For more information, please see **securefreedom.org**

Contents

The Perilous Nexus

FRANK J. GAFFNEY, JR.

T oday, there is growing and increasingly unmistakable evidence of the existence of a nexus between energy and security. The latter should be properly understood to include economic and environmental security, as well as the more traditional aspects of national security. And each is being threatened by serious vulnerabilities associated with America's dependence on foreign supplies of oil.

Frank J. Gaffney, Jr. is the President and CEO of the Center for Security Policy. Mr. Gaffney formerly acted as the Assistant Secretary of Defense for International Security Policy during the Reagan Administration, following four years of service as the Deputy Assistant Secretary of Defense for Nuclear Forces and Arms Control Policy. Mr. Gaffney is host of Secure Freedom Radio.

There are several examples of the ways in which this nexus is being exploited to undermine our security by those who seek to use our energy vulnerability to this country's great detriment.

The most obvious of these is seen in the machinations of the Organization of Petroleum Exporting Countries (OPEC). This cartel dominates, and therefore controls, the production and availability of much of the world's oil, conferring upon it what amounts to a global monopoly. Such control has enabled OPEC for decades to systematically manipulate oil prices—a powerful instrument of economic warfare.

Prior to the financial meltdown, the price of oil was almost one hundred and fifty dollars a barrel. After this meltdown—which was precipitated at least in part by the speculation-driven surge in energy prices—the economic slowdown temporarily drove down the cost per barrel. As recovery has begun to take hold, however, OPEC has inexorably engineered ever-higher prices once again by controlling the amount of oil coming to market. It is predictable that the effect will once again be dire for the US and global economies.

In the past, Russia has also demonstrated an ability and willingness to use energy as a weapon. This is most obviously seen in its coercion of the Ukraine—and, to varying degrees, others among the former Soviet republics that the Kremlin calls the "near-abroad"—powered by cut-offs of Russian natural gas supplies being passed to and/or through such states. Incredibly, this behavior has had no appreciable effect on the willingness of European nations to allow themselves to become increasingly dependent upon gas supplied by Russia. Such a dependency clearly translates into undesirable strategic leverage upon allies of the United States.

There have been many instances in which al-Qaeda has attempted to strike at the key parts of the world's petroleum infrastructure, most notably in Saudi Arabia. In recent years, terrorist attacks that would have immediately and severely disrupted the flow of oil to world markets were narrowly averted.

Recent conflicts have underscored the US military's critical dependence on oil to support its combat and other operations. Among other things, transportation of massive quantities of petroleum to forward operating bases constitutes a formidable logistical problem, as well as a very significant operational liability.

This Achilles' heel is made all the more perilous by the nation's dependence on foreign suppliers of petroleum. Some of these oil exporters are hostile to America's use of force in the Middle East or would become so should their autocratic rulers be replaced by Islamists with even greater antipathy to infidel nations like the United States.

Another issue bearing on the nexus between energy and security arises from the UN Law of the Sea Treaty (LOST)—a prime example of the phenomenon known as "lawfare." This is a term coined to describe the use of international treaties, judicial rulings, "norms," etc., by those hostile to and seeking to subvert American sovereignty. Like the George W. Bush administration before it, the Obama administration seeks US ratification the Law of the Sea Treaty.

Should that happen, there would be several predictable and adverse effects for American energy and national security. For example, should US oil and gas industries seek to exploit energy resources in international waters, they would be subjected to permitting obligations and mechanisms controlled by international bureaucrats, many of whom may prove intensely hostile to this country.

In any event—whether such hostility exists or not in practice— the Law of the Sea Treaty will require these domestic companies to engage in unprecedented transfers of technology and proprietary information to other parties, in this case LOST's International Seabed Authority (ISA) and a mechanism it operates with the Orwellian name of "the Enterprise."

Here's how it is supposed to work under the Law of the Sea Treaty: To get an international permit from the ISA, the would-be developer of, say, deep-ocean oil reserves must identify not one but *two* sites whose potential has been established through sensitive proprietary techniques. The ISA will then determine which of the two the company will be allowed to develop. The other will be turned over to a competitor working for the Enterprise, together with all the necessary data and technology to do such development, which the applicant company will be forced to surrender.

Successful oil and gas corporations do not share that sort of information within their own companies, let alone with their competitors. As a result, it seems unlikely that such American enterprises will agree to subject themselves to such an arrangement in the event that the US Senate actually agrees to the ratification of the Law of the Sea Treaty.

The result would likely be to deny this country access to valuable energy resources that will become ever more vital to our security as sources elsewhere dry up or otherwise become less available. (Of course, those burdensome arrangements and real costs would not apply—and the deep sea resources could be exploited at will—

as long as the United States does not ratify and is not bound by the treaty.)

Worse yet, US ratification of the Law of the Sea Treaty would enable international judges and bureaucrats to engage in lawfare against the United States by promulgating and wielding against us sweeping environmental regulations. Think of them as the Kyoto Protocol on steroids. Such officials will be able not only to exercise control over activities in, under and above international waters, but—on the pretext that any water or air emanates from a sovereign nation—to the interior of member states, as well.

As a result, the oil and gas industry (among many other industries) operating inside the United States, will find themselves subject to regulatory arrangements handed down from wholly unaccountable foreign entities and individuals who do not have America's best interests at heart. We have had a taste of this agenda even in the absence of US ratification of the Law of the Sea Treaty with the suing of Chevron for billions of dollars in penalties for its activities in Ecuador.

Then, there are the ominous implications for US energy and national security associated with the so-called "cap-and-trade" legislation. This initiative represents an unprecedented and immense tax on basically anything having carbon in it, which of course includes much of the energy consumed by the United States. It is foolish and irresponsible to assume that such a massive burden in the absence of vastly more conclusive evidence that such consumption is contributing to catastrophic global warming, or even that such warming is occurring. As of this writing, though, the Democratic-controlled Congress may nonetheless try to impose this sort of tax—with untold consequences for the economy, the nation as a whole and, yes, even its security.

Fortunately, in the face of these ominous developments, there is something that is near-term, practical, technologically feasible and highly affordable that can be done to reduce our vulnerability to OPEC's monopoly and improve markedly our energy security. It is called the Open Fuel Standard (OFS), an idea that is as elegant in its simplicity as it is consequential in its application.

The OFS would require, over time, a growing percentage of new cars sold in America to offer drivers in this country something the vast majority of them lack today: fuel choice. Taking advantage of a well-established and low-cost technology, such cars would be Flexible Fuel Vehicles (FFVs)—automobiles configured to be powered not only by gasoline but by ethanol, methanol, butanol and other alcohol-based fuels, either exclusively or in some combination.

Legislation now awaiting congressional action that would establish this Open Fuel Standard builds upon a commitment that has already been made by what used to be called America's "Big Three"—Ford, Chrysler and General Motors. These companies voluntarily pledged several years ago to then-President Bush that, by 2012, fifty percent of their new car offerings would be FFVs. The legislation would require that that percentage be ramped up to eighty percent by 2015.

Over time, the OFS would transform America's transportation sector from what I call "gasoholic" vehicles to "omnivores." As new FFVs become ever more widely available and older, gas-only cars are phased out, the United States would create a vast new market for fuels that can be produced domestically, in the case of methanol derived from anything made up of carbon. Among such plentiful sources are switchgrass and other plants, wood pulp, used tires and trash.

In this fashion, at the cost of just $100 or less per newly manufactured vehicle, the United States can, over time, wean itself from what amounts to its present, utter dependency on a single source of transportation fuel—oil—most of which is supplied by members of the OPEC cartel. This will have a truly revolutionary strategic effect, especially if, as a practical matter, the US Open Fuel Standard winds up becoming an international standard. That would seem to be a predictable result since car companies, having retooled their production lines to make Flexible Fuel Vehicles, will find it more economical to manufacture basically the same vehicles for sale elsewhere.

As a result, within relatively short order, something like 120 countries around the world, many of them currently desperately poor and unable to afford high gas prices, will be able to produce their own transportation fuels from native vegetation or other sources. Some may even be able to become net energy exporters, offering them a way out of their state of impoverishment.

The result will be the end of OPEC's monopoly and, perhaps, of the cartel itself. In due course, the wherewithal to promote the toxic, totalitarian program authoritative Islam calls "Shariah" and the jihad designed to impose it worldwide—much of it derived from our petrodollar wealth transfers to some of the cartel's most prominent members—will become a thing of the past.

Diversifying fuel supplies will also have a great effect on the military. If even some of our troops' various vehicles can be configured to operate effectively on alcohol-based fuels, it may be possible to produce such fuels in sufficient quantity in the field. In addition to decreasing our dependence on oil and the costs associated therewith, the US armed forces could dramatically reduce some of the yawning infrastructural and logistical problems that currently complicate its operations around the world.

An insight into just how serious those problems are is evident from a single fact: In the course of the campaign to liberate Iraq, the United States military consumed more fuel than in the entire course of its combat operations in Europe during World War II. Such consumption is unsustainable, as are the costs entailed in assuring our access to and movement of petroleum around the world.

Another promising technique for reducing our present need for oil has been developed by Ricardo Incorporated, an innovative, Detroit-based high-tech company, that has developed an engine dubbed an "ethanol-boosted direct-injection engine." This next-generation engine not only takes advantage of and exploits the higher octane of ethanol and methanol to get better fuel efficiency. It also enables a reduction of roughly half the size and weight of current engines, without sacrificing performance. These attributes could be of enormous benefit particularly to the US military if its manned and unmanned vehicles could be made not only much more fuel efficient, but perhaps significantly smaller without sacrificing their effectiveness.

The Obama administration—including both Secretary of Energy Stephen Chu and President Obama, himself—has signaled its support for the Open Fuel Standard. Yet, to date, the legislation needed to establish the OFS has not moved through Congress. Similarly, technology like the Ricardo next-generation engine is not being exploited as aggressively as it could be due to the lack of relatively trivial amounts of funding needed to complete its development.

Which brings us back to the various vulnerabilities arising from the nexus between energy and national security enumerated above. In the event someone seeks to exploit those vulnerabilities by disrupting, through one means or another, US access to oil from overseas, the United States will find itself in a desperate position, seeking alternative sources of energy on a crash basis. Clearly, it will be vastly more difficult to develop and adopt such alternatives under those circumstances than it would be to do so today. We dare not allow that to happen and must implement some of the strategies outlined in this book to ensure that it does not. [1]

Oil's 150th Anniversary: Who's Happy Birthday?

GAL LUFT

O ne hundred and fifty years ago, on August 27, 1859 Colonel Edwin Drake struck oil in Titusville, Pennsylvania, giving rise to the modern oil industry. What was sought as a replacement for depleting stocks of whale oil used as a fuel for lamps, gradually turned into the world's most strategic commodity. Today oil supplies 40% of global energy.

During its century-and-a-half long history, oil has been a source of both prosperity and global volatility.

Petroleum has enabled the production of industrial chemicals, heating oil, medi-

Gal Luft is executive director of the Institute for the Analysis of Global Security (IAGS) and publisher of the Journal of Energy Security, in which this article originally appeared in 2009. He is a co-author of Energy Security Challenges for the 21st Century (Praeger 2009).

cines, plastics, asphalt and lubricants, all of them critical to our modern society. (Contrary to popular belief, the US uses very little oil today to make electricity. At present, only 2% of US electricity is generated from oil.) Most importantly, oil has enabled mobility, and hence a rapid flow of goods and services. This is perhaps the key contributing factor to the impressive global economic growth of the 20th century. Today, roughly two-thirds of the world's oil is used for transportation. Petroleum enjoys a near monopoly in this sector—most of the world's cars, trucks, planes, ships and trains are able to run on nothing else.

On the other side of the balance sheet, global economic dependence on oil and its products has bred considerable trouble. Oil became a backdrop behind great powers' foreign policies and has been a driver of some of the past century's most seminal events.

Imperial Japan's insatiable need for oil led it to adopt in the 1930s an expansionist policy that triggered an oil embargo by the US, then supplier of 80% of the island nation's oil imports. Tokyo's response, sending its navy to attack Pearl Harbor, provoked a four-year war in the Pacific which took two mushroom clouds to end. In Europe, Nazi Germany's need for oil compelled Adolf Hitler to invade Russia and later to divert his Panzers from Moscow to the Soviet oil center in Baku, a decision that sealed the fate of the Third Reich.

With the war's end, attention shifted to the Middle East as the world's most important source of oil and the key to the stability of the global economy. Today, this tumultuous region produces nearly 40% of the world's oil and is home to two-thirds of proven global conventional oil reserves and to over half of undiscovered reserves. Since the historic February 1945 meeting aboard the USS Quincy between the ailing US President Franklin D. Roosevelt and King Abdul Aziz ibn Saud of Saudi Arabia, oil considerations have governed US Middle East policy, and the US has considered it essential to engage in military activity in order to ensure continued access to the Persian Gulf.

The Carter Doctrine, the "reflagging" of Kuwaiti tankers during the Iran-Iraq War, the 1991 Gulf War and US military presence in Saudi Arabia, Qatar, Bahrain, Kuwait and, most recently, Iraq, have all been tied to America's energy security needs.

For the US, the dependence on oil comes at a cost. It has forced Washington to establish "special relations" with non-democratic and unpopular regimes, such as those of the Shah of

Iran and the House of Saud, while US military presence in the region has been a lightning rod for the region's radicals.

In February 2005, President George W. Bush conceded that "The policy in the past used to be, let's just accept tyranny, for the sake of [...] cheap oil [...] and just hope everything would be okay. Well, that changed on September the 11th. Everything wasn't okay. Beneath what appeared to be a placid surface lurked an ideology based upon hatred."

Also on the negative side, the global oil industry is more than ever a government-dominated business. More than 80% of the world's reserves are controlled by governments and their proxies, and what was once the privately-owned Seven Sisters are now seven midgets in comparison to the 'new Seven Sisters,' all government run: Saudi Aramco, Russia's Gazprom, China's CNPC, Iran's NIOC, Venezuela's PDVSA, Brazil's Petrobras and Malaysia's Petronas. Such government control over the world's fuel supply makes oil a tool of foreign policy which was clearly demonstrated during the 1973 Arab oil embargo.

A world of high oil prices is a poison pill for everything the US and its allies are trying to accomplish abroad from democracy promotion and human rights protection to counter-proliferation of terrorism and nuclear weapons. With few exceptions, oil exporting countries' human rights records leave much to be desired. Only 10% of the world's proven reserves are concentrated in countries ranked "free" by Freedom House. In many countries highly dependent on oil revenues for their income, such as Sudan, Azerbaijan, Kazakhstan, Saudi Arabia, Iran, Angola, Nigeria, Chad, Venezuela and Russia, high oil prices enable authoritarian regimes to consolidate their power and erode progress toward freedom and democracy.

As a result, in many parts of the world, millions of people have been enslaved, oppressed and denied basic freedoms by non-democratic oil regimes aided by the silence of the importers who depend upon them. Then Secretary of State Condoleezza Rice in 2006 offered Senators telling testimony revealing the depth of frustration with the toxic influence oil dependence has on America's foreign policy: "nothing has really taken me aback more, as Secretary of State, than the way that the politics of energy is [...] 'warping' diplomacy around the world."

Redefining Energy Independence

T he array of security, economic and environmental challenges associated with US oil dependence have popularized the call for "energy independence" beyond any other issue in America's political discourse. Public opinion polls show that Americans, regardless of their political affiliation, see energy independence as an urgent imperative.

President Barack Obama's first budget proposal was tied to a renewable energy program "to help the US move toward energy independence." Yet, despite its popular appeal, in many circles the concept is met with scepticism—in some cases outright contempt. Energy independence has been referred to as a "pipe dream," a "misguided quest" and a "dangerous illusion." A Council on Foreign Relations task force went so far as to accuse those promoting energy independence of "doing the nation a disservice." The critics' skepticism stems from their literal interpretation of the concept: they view "independence" as self-sufficiency, or not importing oil even though the US remains dependent on it.

Under this interpretation, energy independence is indeed unattainable. The US consumes about 21 million barrels per day, 60% of which are imported. If these barrels were attached to each other they would make a pipe long enough to connect New York and Beijing. For a country that owns barely 3% of the world's conventional oil reserves, replacing such a vast amount of oil with domestic resources is "mission impossible."

But self-sufficiency is not what independence means. The problem of oil dependence is not about the amount of oil consumed or imported. The problem is that oil is a strategic commodity by virtue of its virtual monopoly over transportation fuel. This monopoly gives a small group of nations inordinate power on the world stage. "Independence" as *Webster's Dictionary* says, is "not being subject to control by others," or in our case, being a free actor by reducing the role of oil in world politics—turning it from a strategic commodity into one interchangeable with others.

This is exactly what happened to another commodity which was once monopolized, and considered critical to humanity's functioning: salt. Odd as it seems, for centuries salt mines conferred national power. Wars were fought over salt. Colonies were formed in remote places where it happened to be found. That was because salt had a virtual monopoly over food preservation. With the advent of canning, electricity, and refrigeration, salt lost its strategic status, and salt rich domains like Orissa, Tortuga and Boa Vista that once held as much sway as today's Gulf Emirates are no longer places of strategic importance. Countries still use, import, and trade salt, but salt is no longer a commodity that dictates world affairs. Turning oil into salt is what energy independence is all about.

When in a Hole, Stop Digging

Oil's monopoly over transportation fuel is complicated by the fact that this monopoly is also married to a cartel.

During the past four decades, members of the Organization of Petroleum Exporting Countries (OPEC), which collectively sit atop 78% of world oil reserves, have been producing far less than their geological endowment permits. In 1973, just before the Arab Oil Embargo, OPEC produced 30 million barrels per day. Thirty-six years later, with global demand and non-OPEC production having nearly doubled, and despite the fact that in 2007 the cartel swallowed two new members—Angola and Ecuador—with combined daily production capacity equivalent to that of Norway, OPEC's crude production has not increased. In fact, in 2009 it is expected to average 29 million barrels a day—less than in 1973.

For OPEC, oil's 150th anniversary is a somber one. It comes at a time of deep global recession which has shaved $100 per barrel off the historically high price oil hit last summer. Persian Gulf economies have been dealt painful blows by oil output cuts, heavy losses in their sovereign wealth funds and weak consumer demand. The cartel's revenues in 2009 are projected to fall by more than 60% from last year's one trillion dollar income. If the recession is prolonged, we could see the first signs of social discontent leading to political reverberations in petrodollar dependent economies.

Adding to the producers' angst are the repeated calls for energy independence coming from Washington's political class and the Obama Administration's signals that the US would be part of a post -Kyoto climate agreement which would impose an additional cost on use of hydrocarbons. This leaves little appetite among producers to invest the billions of dollars necessary to prepare the oil industry for the post-recession era.

The International Energy Agency (IEA) recently concluded that even with the current recession, by 2030 global demand for oil could increase by 25%. At the same time, the agency examined the status of the world's 800 top oilfields and reported an average annual depletion rate of 5.5% increasing to 8.6% in 2030. In order to meet future projected demand for oil, four new Saudi Arabias will have to be added to the global oil market between now and 2030. But the current economic conditions have thwarted the much needed investment in new production.

According to OPEC, since last year, 35 major exploration projects have been shelved. Ali al Naimi, the Saudi oil minister, during the March OPEC meeting warned of a coming "catastrophic" shortfall in petroleum production, raising doubts the world can count on the one Saudi Arabia that exists, not the least on the four that don't.

Failure by producers to prepare the ground for the post-recession era could cause a severe oil-price shock reminiscent of that in 2008 once the economy recovers and demand for liquid fuels surges. This could, in turn, send the world into a new round of economic turmoil, leading to a W-shaped, double dipped, recovery instead of a traditional V-shaped recovery in which economic growth bounces back quickly from a slump.

And yet, despite the geological, strategic, economic, and environmental indicators showing that in the coming decades the cost of maintaining the oil economy will grow exponentially, we ignore the dictum: "when in a hole, stop digging." Every year more than 50 million new petroleum-only cars roll onto the planet's roads, each with an average street life of 15 years, hence locking humanity's future to petroleum exporting nations and their whims for many years to come.

The recent introduction of the $2,000 Tata Nano, the world's cheapest car, which aims to fulfill the aspirations for fast mobility of hundreds of millions of potential motorists in the developing world, is the latest manifestation of the mismatch between the growing number of gasoline-only vehicle platforms produced worldwide and the ability of the oil industry to power them.

From Monopoly to Fuel Choice

Addressing the energy security challenge requires an understanding that much touted policies that aim to either increase oil supply through domestic drilling or the ones that decrease its use by boosting fuel efficiency, while helpful, are insufficient as they ignore the main enabler of the oil monopoly: the petroleum-only vehicle. In fact, experience of the past three decades shows that whenever non-OPEC producers increase their production, OPEC decreases supply accordingly. Similarly, when demand for oil drops OPEC quickly responds with production cuts.

In other words, when we drill more, OPEC drills less; when we use less, OPEC drills less. Changing this vexing dynamic requires competition and fuel choice in the transportation sector which can only be achieved if new vehicles are built as platforms on which other fuels can compete.

A few types of vehicle technologies already offer such a possibility. The first, and most affordable, is the flex-fuel vehicle that can run on any combination of gasoline and alcohol (alcohol does not mean just ethanol, and ethanol does not mean just corn).

The technology is a century old. Henry Ford's Model T was a flex-fuel vehicle. It costs an extra $100 per new car to make a regular car flex-fuel. All it takes is a fuel sensor and a corrosion-resistant fuel line, because alcohol is more corrosive than gasoline. In 2008, 80% of the new cars sold in Brazil were flexible-fuel vehicles. This opened the once petroleum dominated transportation fuel market to competition. Between 2005 and 2008 while fuel prices nearly doubled everywhere, in Brazil—where ethanol is cheaply made from sugarcane—they were almost frozen. When oil prices soared in 2008, ethanol became so popular in Brazil that gasoline became an "alternative fuel."

Another big country that seems to be on its way to adopt the Brazilian model of fuel flexibility is China. Since 1993, the year it became a net oil importer, China's oil imports have grown by leaps and bounds. China imports nearly half of its oil, and it recently passed Japan to become the world's second largest oil importing nation after the US.

Until 2006, China invested in expanding its ethanol industry to become the world's third-largest ethanol producer, behind Brazil and the US. But with soaring food prices in 2006, the Chinese government hit the brakes and banned the use of grain for alcohol production. With no hyperactive farm lobby nor Iowa caucuses, China decided to veer toward another alcohol—methanol.

The distinction between methanol (wood alcohol) and ethanol (grain alcohol) is for many akin to the difference between Iran and Iraq—but one letter makes all the difference. Ethanol can be made from agricultural products like corn, sugar cane, sugar beet and cellulosic material like switch grass, wood chips and other agricultural and forest residue. Methanol can be made from all of the above plus an array of other energy sources including natural gas, coal, garbage and even carbon dioxide—one elegant way to address greenhouse gas emissions.

Because of methanol's scalability, China's leading automakers are gearing up to produce methanol-enabled flex-fuel cars which can run on gasoline, ethanol and methanol in any combination. For the ailing US auto industry, making fuel flexibility a standard feature in every new vehicle would be as technologically and financially manageable as were the introductions of similar features like seatbelts, airbags or rear view mirrors. Many of the flex-fuel cars sold in Brazil are made by General Motors and Ford.

An Open Fuel Standard requiring that every new car sold in the US be flex-fuel would not only give rise to an industry of alternative fuels and the associated refuelling infrastructure, but it would also compel foreign automobile makers to add fuel flexibility to all of their models, effectively making it an international standard.

Shifting to alcohol production from non-food biomass material like dedicated grasses, algae and forestry waste could enable scaled production to the tune of tens of billions of gallons in the US alone. According to a 2009 study by Sandia National Laboratories, greater productivity of cellulosic feedstock should eventually allow biomass-based alcohol to displace nearly a third of all gasoline use by 2030.

An even bigger potential for biomass production exists in the poor countries of Africa, Latin America and South Asia with their strong agricultural base and massive endowment of arable land. By cultivating their agricultural base to grow energy crops, provided that such an expansion is done in a sustainable manner, such countries—many of them on the receiving end of US development aid—would be empowered economically as they become net fuel exporters. This would improve their trade balance, create jobs and spare them the need to import expensive oil for their own economies.

Natural gas converted into methanol can also be used to power flexible-fuel cars. About a third of the world's emissions of methane, a greenhouse gas 23 times more potent than CO_2, occur in coal mines and natural gas wells. According to the World Bank sponsored Global Gas Flaring Reduction Partnership, five trillion cubic feet of natural gas are being flared annually by oil companies, equivalent to 27% of total US natural gas consumption. Using as little as 10% of this gas would produce enough methanol to fuel five million cars.

For some countries compressed natural gas is already being used as a gasoline alternative on board bi-fuel vehicles. These cars have two fuels, liquids and gas, stored in separate tanks—and the engine runs on one fuel at a time. India, with the fifth largest fleet of natural gas vehicles in the world, probably holds the highest potential for growth. Two thousand refuelling stations are now being planned for construction and more than 220 cities are projected to be connected to a nationwide distribution pipeline system. Interestingly, two of the leading countries in natural gas vehicle deployment are Venezuela and Iran.

In both, significant parts of domestic auto sales are mandated to be natural gas enabled; hundreds of natural gas fuelling stations are being built as well as conversion centers which allow drivers to retrofit their gasoline-only cars to also run on natural gas.

For countries like Iran and Venezuela that keep fuel costs artificially low even when prices rise, the shift to natural gas is a way to avoid the socially destabilizing removal of fuel subsidies. For Iran, there is also a strategic imperative. Due to lack of refining capacity, forty percent of Iran's gasoline is imported. As the world's second largest reserve of natural gas, Iran could become independent of imported gas and hence immune to sanctions.

Whether or not the US should emulate Iran, Venezuela, India and a handful of other countries which have decided to pit natural gas against oil at the pump is a matter of debate.

American oilman T. Boone Pickens thinks this is a good idea, claiming that natural gas can displace thirty percent of US oil imports. Others doubt the wisdom of "jumping from the frying pan into the fire" by trading dependence on one commodity, the bulk of which is controlled by problematic regimes united in a cartel, with another that exhibits the exact same challenges and whose top exporters—Russia, Iran, Algeria and Qatar—are already in discussions about the formation of an OPEC like natural gas cartel. But whether or not the US is to adopt this option, worldwide, this source of energy is already displacing an ever increasing amount of petroleum.

Electricity used as a transportation fuel could displace a large amount of oil. It is cheap, domestically produced and can be made from multiple sources. Its refuelling infrastructure is widely available. All that is needed for an electric car to connect to the grid is an extension cord.

Most automakers have already committed to produce models of pure electric vehicles (EV) or plug-in hybrid electric vehicles (PHEV), essentially hybrid cars with a larger battery and a plug. This system allows the driver to drive on stored electric power for the first 20-40 miles, depending on the battery size, after which the car keeps running on the liquid fuel in the tank, providing the standard three or four hundred mile range drivers are accustomed to.

For the 50% of Americans who drive 25 miles per day or less, shifting from barrels to electrons would make the visit to the local gas station a rarity, assuming they plugged their car in the night before. If all of those Americans owned PHEVs, a population the size of New York, Florida and Pennsylvania combined would be off oil most days of the year.

A PHEV would normally drive 100-150 miles per gallon. If it is also made as flex-fuel and is powered by 85% alcohol and 15% gasoline, each gallon of petroleum is stretched with alcohol fuel by a factor of five, and oil economy could reach over 500 miles per gallon of gasoline. As former Saudi oil minister Sheikh Ahmed Zaki Yamani observed nine years ago, "technology is a real enemy for OPEC."

A Looming Face-off

The pace of market diffusion of new transportation technologies leaves no doubt that in the coming years the transportation sector will become decreasingly captive to oil. Petroleum exporting countries wishing to prolong the economic system on which they thrive will be forced to fight for their market share in the face of deepening cracks in their strategic dominance. But for all its challenges, oil is not likely to easily vacate its pedestal, and the arrows in the quiver of its producers are still many.

The world may no longer be awash with conventional oil, but the amount of reserves off-shore and in the universe of non-conventional sources like oil shale and tar sands, can extend oil's play for many years to come, albeit at potentially higher environmental cost. Producers will have to do more to flatten the roller coaster of oil prices seen in recent months mainly through closer coordination between OPEC and Russia, mothballing (preparing oilfields for recovery but not touching them unless there is clear demand) and by increasing spare production capacity. Their fortunes will be bolstered by the non-trivial and often unexpected challenges alternative fuels and advanced automotive technologies will face on their way to mass market penetration. For automakers, flex-fuel capability may be no more than a low cost adjustment in the assembly line.

But while the cars are easily deployable, supplying them with fuel in sufficient quantities to make a dent in the oil economy will be a monumental challenge. Refueling stations would have to retrofit their pumps—today only 2,750 of 170,000 refuelling stations in the US offer alternative fuels—a network of pipelines would have to be built to move the fuel from production facilities to the distribution centers and, most importantly, fuel supply would have to increase in spades. Hundreds of new alternative fuel plants will have to be sited, engineered and built, and a gigantic amount of feedstocks of various sorts will have to be grown, collected and mined. This massive undertaking will take a long time to mount.

Electric transportation poses challenges of its own. The fuel and the refuelling infrastructure are relatively easy to obtain but the vehicle ramp up is costly and slow.

Consider this: even if industry succeeded in meeting President Obama's goal and deployed one million PHEVs by 2015, this would barely constitute one half of one percent of the US auto fleet. Electric motors may be cheap, reliable and easy to manufacture but the rechargeable batteries needed to power them still face hurdles on the road to mass production related to their capacity, safety, reliability, longevity and, perhaps most challenging, cost. Depending on the size, a Lithium Ion battery, the leading battery chemistry to power PHEVs, costs $8,000-$15,000 (roughly $1,000/kWh) while a 30kWh battery needed to power an EV costs about $18,000 ($600/kWh).

To prevent such cars from becoming money losers, their battery cost should come down to under $300/kWh. Notwithstanding the impressive progress that has been made in recent years in ro chargeable battery manufacturing and the US Congress' recent allocation of $2.4 billion in taxpayers' funds to produce PHEVs and advanced battery components, the US is nowhere near being a global leader in battery manufacturing.

Last year Japan produced 39% of the world's supply of advanced lithium-ion batteries, China 36%, South Korea 20% and 5% was shared by the rest of the world including the US.

As importers chart their way away from oil, they will likely discover that along with the geopolitical benefits associated with such a shift come new challenges of growing dependence on alternative commodities. While Asia controls the market for advanced batteries, South America is the source of the materials from which batteries are made. More than 80% of the world's reserve base of lithium is concentrated in South America. Bolivia, a drug producing country that last year expelled its US ambassador, owns nearly half of the world's economically recoverable lithium.

Shifting the epicenter of the world's energy system from the Persian Gulf to East Asia and South America will over time recalibrate nations' foreign policies, reshuffle political alliances and create new strategic interests as was the case in previous centuries when humanity traded one dependence with another.

Whether or not this new energy landscape will improve America's posture abroad is premature to determine. But from today's vantage point—heading toward a situation in which, in the words of the chief economist of the IEA "95% of the world relying for its economic well-being on decisions made by five or six countries in the Middle East"—such over-the-horizon risk seems worth taking. The prospects of a nuclear Middle East, with massive youth bulges, lurking social discontent and persistent oppression, holding the key to global mobility should be enough of an impetus to ensure that on its 200th anniversary oil be no more central to the world economy than salt is today. [1]

In Defense of Biofuels

ROBERT ZUBRIN

O n the world markets, the price of a barrel of oil during 2008 averaged $110/barrel. As a result, the United States, which imports 5 billion barrels of oil per year, was presented with a 2008 petroleum bill topping $600 billion for foreign oil, plus $400 billion more for domestic oil. This trillion dollar drain on the US economy—equal to 40 percent of the sum that Americans pay in federal taxes—not only caused record gasoline prices, but drove the nation (and most of the rest of the world, looted of $4 trillion in total) deep into recession.

Dr. Robert Zubrin, a Senior Fellow with the Center for Security Policy, is President of Pioneer Astronautics, an aerospace engineering R&D company, and the author of *Energy Victory: Winning the War on Terror by Breaking Free of Oil*. This piece was initially published in *The New Atlantis* in 2008, and was adapted by the author for purposes of this volume.

With less cash available to spend on houses, real estate markets collapsed, destroying mortgage values and endangering major financial institutions in the process. With less cash available for retail purchases, sales fell off on everything from automobiles to cappuccino, forcing businesses to close down or lay off workers, increasing unemployment and cutting government revenues. As a result, the federal deficit rose first to a record $500 billion, and then soared to an incredible $2 trillion as the government haplessly threw cash in all directions to try to avert a total financial collapse.

And yet, bizarrely, instead of focusing their attention on the staggering cost of oil and its ruinous implications for economic growth and well being, a host of commentators have begun to decry a different fuel—one that holds the key to ending our dependency on expensive oil purchased from countries with interests inimical to our own.

Biofuels—a class of fuels of which ethanol is the most prominent and immediately promising—can play a central part in weaning the United States from oil. But starting in early 2008, when the price of oil first crossed the $100/bbl threshold, a flood of press reports, articles in scientific journals, and statements from international bureaucrats deluged the media suggesting that ethanol is starving the world's poor, is a waste of government money, and is bad for the environment. These claims are simply not true; some are based on partial information, some on gross disinformation, but none of them can withstand close scrutiny.

Many of the critics of ethanol may mean well: they are worried about the diversion of food grains from hungry children, or the costs of government biofuel subsidies to the taxpayer. Other members of the anti-ethanol chorus though, have more self-interested motivations for their criticism of biofuels, including Saudi oil minister Ali bin Ibrahim Al-Naimi[1], OPEC president (and Algerian Energy Minister) Chakib Khelil[2], and, most vigorously, Venezuelan dictator Hugo Chávez[3], an ardent proponent of high oil prices, who called ethanol production a "crime." Indeed, for those in the know, it hardly came as a surprise when it was revealed that the Glover Park public relations firm, which is registered with the US Department of Justice[4] as an agent of the United Arab Emirates, was heavily involved in orchestrating the anti-ethanol campaign.[5] Then there were still others, not apparently connected to the oil interest, whose opposition to ethanol—and agriculture in general—seems to be driven by a Malthusian vision of a world with fewer people in it. No matter the motivations of these unlikeliest of bedfellows, their recent objections to ethanol threaten to have the cumulative effect of warping US and international biofuels policy—and just at the moment when exorbitant oil costs should, if anything, be leading legislators to adopt the critical technology needed to expand the role of biofuels in the world's fuel supply.

Fueling Rumors About Food

Hoping to reduce at least in some small way their need for oil, several countries have adopted energy policies requiring that a percentage of their national fuel supplies consist of biofuels. The European Union, for instance, is aiming to have biofuels make up 10 percent of its vehicle fuel supply by the year 2020. In the United States, legislation in 2005 and 2007 set mandates for ethanol in the nation's fuel mix; the current plan is to ramp up biofuels production until 36 billion gallons are mixed into the nation's fuel supply by 2022.

Unsurprisingly, the result of these mandates has been the rapid expansion of the nation's ethanol industry. The United States, which produced 3 billion gallons of ethanol in 2002, grew its production to 9 billion gallons in 2008, replacing some 6 percent of our gasoline supply. But while this seems like it would be cause for celebration—with enterprising and innovative American farmers helping to reduce our oil usage—some critics have recently alleged that the world's biofuels programs, especially the US corn ethanol effort, are starving poor people around the world by reducing supply and driving up prices. International bureaucrats have been the most vocal critics. A recent World Bank report claimed that "increased biofuel production has contributed to the rise in food prices." The U.N.'s Special Rapporteur on the Right to Food denounced biofuel production as "a crime against humanity." Jeffrey Sachs, a Columbia University economist who is an advisor to U.N. Secretary-General Ban Ki-moon, has said "we need to cut back significantly on our biofuels programs" because they are "a huge blow to the world food supply." It seems so obvious: with so much corn being turned into fuel, food shortages must inevitably result, and biofuel programs must be the cause.

The problem is, that's completely untrue.

Here are the facts. In the last five years, despite the nearly threefold growth of the corn ethanol industry—actually, *because* of it—the amount of corn grown in the United States has vastly increased. The US corn crop grew by 45 percent, the production of distillers grain (a high-value animal feed made from the protein saved from the corn used for ethanol) quadrupled, and the net US corn production of food for humans and feed for animals increased 34 percent.

Contrary to claims that farmers have cut other crops to grow more corn, US soybean plantings in 2008 were up 18 percent and wheat plantings up 6 percent. US farm exports are up 23 percent over 2007. America is clearly doing its share in feeding the world.

Agriculture is not a zero-sum game. There are roughly 2,250 million acres of land in the continental United States. About 1,600 million of those acres are arable. Roughly half of that land (800 million acres) is farmland, but only about a third of that (280 million acres) is actually being cultivated. Only about 85 million of those farm acres are presently growing corn, and just a fifth of *that* land—about 17 million acres—is growing corn that becomes ethanol. In short, there is plenty of farmland in the United States that could be used to grow more corn—or more of the other staple crops needed to meet domestic or international demand. In fact, the federal government, through the Department of Agriculture's Conservation Reserve Program, actually pays American farmers *not to farm* scores of millions of acres of their land.

So while it is true that there is now much more corn being used for ethanol than ever before, there is also much more total corn than ever before, including much more for food and feed than ever before, and still plenty of land to grow yet more.

But if biofuels aren't to blame for the rising food prices, what is?

In fact, there are several culprits. One is low farm productivity in some parts of the world. Regional droughts is another. Sometimes there is a confluence of factors. Some critics have foolishly claimed that recent food riots in Haiti could be linked to the US ethanol mandate even though those riots were about rice, which the US doesn't use to make ethanol, and were largely caused by unwise trade policies and a drought in Australia that, according to the *St. Petersburg Times*, "has seen [its] rice production fall by a stunning 98 percent."

But the two primary reasons for higher food prices are, first, higher demand, and second, higher fuel prices. The increased global demand for food ought to be seen as a very good thing: it represents hundreds of millions of people, especially in China and India, rising out of poverty and moving to more calorie-rich diets. Escalating fuel prices, however, are not good news: they drive up the cost of every-thing we eat. For example, consider the $3 box of cornflakes you might see in your grocery store. Farm commodity prices basically have a trivial effect on its price. A bushel of corn contains 56 pounds of grain, so at the 2008 maximum "very high" commodity price of $7 per bushel, a pound of corn went for 12 cents. So at the 2008 maximum price, the 16 ounces of corn in that cereal box cost a total of 12 cents when bought from the farmer. But when the price of oil goes up, that increases the cost of production, transport, wages, and packaging—all driving up the retail cost of food. (It should be noted that, since 2008, the corn commodity price has fallen to $4/bushel, despite further increases in ethanol production.)

And, in this regard, biofuels have already done more good than harm to the world's poor. According to the *Wall Street Journal*, "Global production of biofuels is rising annually by the equivalent of about 300,000 barrels of oil a day. That goes a long way toward meeting the growing demand for oil, which last year rose by about 900,000 barrels a day." The paper cites a Merrill Lynch analyst who "says that oil and gasoline prices would be about 15 percent higher if biofuel producers weren't increasing their output." So even though the world's biofuels industry is still just aborning, it has al-ready begun to bring down oil prices.

Why Adam Smith Would Love Ethanol

T hat figure from Merrill Lynch contains within it the rebuttal to those who believe the United States should give up on ethanol. Those critics are mostly well-meaning small-government conservatives and libertarians who generally oppose government mandates and subsidies—an honorable disposition, to be sure, but one that must not be followed blindly. They have called for the United States to drop its mandates for incorporating ethanol into the nation's fuel supply, and have used the recent anti-biofuels push to repeat their longstanding complaints about the federal gov-ernment's subsidies for biofuels.

But if that Merrill Lynch figure is correct—if the price of oil would be about 15 percent higher were it not for biofuels—then that comes to a savings of about $18 per barrel at 2008 oil prices. The United States will import about 5 billion barrels of oil this year. Saving $18 for each barrel, that adds up to a savings for the country as a whole of $90 billion in foreign oil payments per year, and a reduction in OPEC global revenues overall of more that $180 billion. This is in addition to cutting another $20 billion from our oil bill by reducing the amount of petroleum that we import. Not bad considering the pittance that American taxpayers actually shell out for the nation's corn ethanol program: only about $4 billion per year, through a subsidy of 45 cents per gallon.

And that isn't the only way that the ethanol subsidy saves taxpayers money—it also allows for the elimination of $8 billion in government-funded crop price supports.

Again, many of the opponents of mandates and subsidies are honorable critics, troubled by government interference distorting the markets for food and energy. But it must be remembered: the global markets for food and energy are already badly distorted by trade restrictions, in the case of the former, and by the machinations of the OPEC cartel, in the case of the latter. Insofar as the nascent biofuels industry will result in eased trade restrictions (so that nations will be able to buy and sell agricultural products for fuel) and in a weakening of OPEC's monopoly power (by bringing into the energy market new fuels that can compete with oil), supporters of free markets should offer three cheers for the rise of biofuels.

It is worth mentioning that Adam Smith, the patron saint of capitalism, was not blindly in favor of markets. Despite his general support for free trade, he wrote in *The Wealth of Nations* that he favored protectionism in cases "when some particular sort of industry is necessary for the defense of the country." After all, "defense is of much more importance than opulence." In fact, he didn't just favor trade restrictions—he even supported subsidies for the sake of national defense: "If any particular manufacture was necessary, indeed, for the defense of the society," Smith wrote, "it might not always be prudent to depend upon our neighbors for the supply; and if such manufacture could not otherwise be supported at home, it might not be unreasonable that all the other branches of industry should be taxed in order to support it." In particular, Smith pointed to the British sailcloth industry—vital to naval propulsion in his day—as eminently deserving of government subsidy. Our need for fuel supplies independent of those imported from unfriendly nations is patently a matter of national defense, and Adam Smith would surely smile benevolently upon the federal government's support of the biofuels industry—as should anyone interested in America's prosperity and security.

Omissions and Emissions

For years, the environmental movement supported the US ethanol program on the grounds that, by replacing oil with fuel made from biomass, we could reduce the nation's net emissions of the greenhouse gas carbon dioxide. That support has wavered recently, thanks primarily to a new study claiming to show the opposite—that the US corn ethanol program actually produces *more* greenhouse gases than would be entailed just by making an equivalent amount of fuel using petroleum, and thus should be condemned by all right-thinking people.

Well, as the saying goes, a lie can circle the globe in the time it takes truth to put her boots on. While it continues to be cited endlessly in the press—and was an impetus for *Time* magazine's sensationalistic recent decision to brand biofuels a "scam"—the study is a Grade A example of junk science.

The study, which appeared in the journal *Science*, was authored by a team led by Timothy Searchinger, presently affiliated with Princeton University's Woodrow Wilson School.[6] Searchinger, it is worth noting, is not a scientist; he is a lawyer who worked, until recently, for Environmental Defense, the organization best known for the role it played in banning the pesticide DDT in the 1970s—a ban that has resulted in millions of African children dying from malaria.

The Searchinger study offers no new data concerning the US corn ethanol program, conceding—in agreement with numerous previous studies—that the ethanol program's *direct effects* will reduce the nation's greenhouse gas emissions by replacing oil with fuel derived from biomass. However, it then goes on to argue that if *indirect effects* are taken into account, including most notably the potential expansion of Third World agriculture in response to the rise of an international market for biofuels, then the overall net effect will be an increase in global greenhouse emissions. Based on a "worldwide agricultural model," the study claims that US agricultural exports will "decline sharply" because more and more American farmland will be used for ethanol—and in order to make up for the lost food supply, Latin American and African peasants will burn down forests to expand farmland. This burning, the study maintains, will put millions of tons of carbon dioxide into the atmosphere, resulting in more emissions than would have come from just burning oil-based fuels.

However the real-world data don't back up these claims. For starters, the Searchinger study's central assumption—that the rising demand for ethanol will lead to a decline in US agricultural exports—is just not true. There has been no reduction in US corn exports, and the US Department of Agriculture projects that corn supplies for food exports, for feed, and for other non-biofuel uses will continue to grow even as ethanol production expands.

Second, Searchinger's study relies on a flawed assumption about the scope of the US corn ethanol program, one in which the US will be producing 30 billion gallons of corn ethanol per year by 2015. But in the very 2007 law that mandated the increased use of biofuels, Congress put a cap on the production of *corn* ethanol—a limit of 15 billion gallons by 2015. This error in the study was pointed out in a devastating online response penned by Michael Wang, a researcher at the Argonne National Laboratory, and Zia Haq, a researcher with the US Department of Energy. Searchinger, they wrote, "examined a corn ethanol production case that is not directly relevant to US corn ethanol production for the next seven years." Wang and Haq's rebuttal is especially powerful since the agricultural model that Searchinger employed was actually first developed by Wang a decade ago.

Third, *contra* Searchinger, there is no evidence that the US corn ethanol program is causing arable land to be cleared elsewhere. To again quote Wang and Haq:

> [Searchinger's assumption about land-use changes] is seriously flawed by predicting deforestation in the Amazon and conversion of grassland into crop land in China, India, and the United States. The fact is, deforestation rates have already declined through legislation in Brazil and elsewhere. In China, contrary to the Searchinger *et al.* assumptions, efforts have been made in the past ten years to convert marginal crop land into grassland and forest land in order to prevent soil erosion and other environmental problems.

To be clear: deforestation is certainly happening—and was happening prior to the advent and expansion of the US corn ethanol program. If it *is* accelerating now, that could be due to any number of causes, including, notably, the high oil prices that the ethanol program serves to combat. The more the global $4 trillion OPEC extortion forces the poor into desperation, the more incentive there will be to cannibalize long term resources such as forests for lumber or firewood.

And beyond these specific flaws in the study's assumptions, the claim of Searchinger and his colleagues to possess a computer model capable of predicting global human behavior must be taken with a grain of salt. While it might be reasonable to suppose that Third World farmers would respond to either high fuel or food prices by clearing more land for agricultural activity, the assumption in the Searchinger study that they would do this by simply burning down their forests—thus creating a "carbon debt" that would take decades or even centuries of biofuel production to "pay back"—is purely speculative.

In fact, most of the Amazon deforestation is being driven , not by agriculture, but by lumbering interests, and should biofuel technology reach the point where either methanol or cellulosic ethanol can be adopted as an economically feasible fuel, then forestry residues would become valuable biofuel resources themselves, and the last thing Third World farmers would want to do would be to burn these enormous revenue sources. Instead they would harvest them, and as their energy content would be used to replace petroleum, there would be no significant "carbon debt."

The Ethic of Envirostasis

Beyond such factual and logical errors, however, the "indirect analysis" methodology used in the Searchinger study is systematically flawed and has nothing in common with the scientific method. Using the same sort of indirect analysis employed by Searchinger—that is, making broad claims of global effects stemming from undemonstrated causal relationships—it is possible to "prove" that increasing mileage standards for vehicles contributes to global warming. Consider: every gallon of gasoline not used by a motorist saves him $2.50 at today's prices. He can use that money to buy other things. For example, at current prices (about $12 per ton), $2.50 could buy him 416 pounds of coal. Burning that coal would obviously produce far more carbon dioxide emissions than burning the 6 pounds of carbon in one gallon of gas. So higher mileage standards for cars cause global warming. Q.E.D.

That is an utterly preposterous conclusion, of course, but it is a decent approximation of the Searchinger team's approach. In fact, using indirect analysis, it is possible to show that *any* technology or policy which can be plausibly argued to confer any social benefit whatsoever will cause global warming. For example, both *tax cuts* (because they give consumers greater spending power) and *tax increases* (because they allow for expanded funding of health care and public education, which in turn contribute to longer lifespans and income growth) can be considered indirect causes of global warming. Perhaps then, we should keep taxes the same? Nope—that won't help a bit, since relative to a potential tax cut, level taxes are a tax increase, and relative to a potential tax increase, level taxes are a tax cut. So keeping tax rates the same will cause global warming through both mechanisms—and thus possibly represents the gravest global warming threat of all.

The point isn't simply that the Searchinger study is wrong, but that it represents a method that can be used to produce any conclusion desired. And the desired conclusions, in Searchinger's case, are shaped by what you might call an ethic of "envirostasis"—the belief that the ultimate measure of the merit of any human activity or innovation is its effect on the climate. This way of thinking is profoundly antihuman, and can lead rapidly to horrific policy prescriptions.

Morality Unhinged

To see just how pernicious such envirostasis-based ethics can be, let us consider vitamins. Prior to the discovery of vitamins, millions of people—especially poor people with limited diets—were weakened or killed by nutritional deficiencies. But now, these people survive, and according to indirect analysis, create a massive global warming effect through their collective carbon footprint. So vitamins are bad, and needless to say, antibiotics are much worse. But even these indirect global warming threats pale before those posed by public sanitation, and clean, safe drinking water. Clearly then, according to envirostasis ethics, all such efforts are to be aborted, and medical research, which threatens to bring more such horrors into the world, should be proscribed.

By indirect analysis, however, not only technological innovations, but the knowledge that fosters them, and the means of disseminating such knowledge, also cause global warming. So, for example, the Google search engine, by making technical information much more available to researchers worldwide, must be seen as a major global warming culprit, and should be shut down, along with the rest of the internet. But we must not stop there, because more traditional methods of disseminating information, including books, magazines (even *Science*), newspapers, libraries, the patent registry, and the postal system, would remain as massive global warming agents—as proven by the fact that global warming began before the internet. So we need to get rid of them too, as well as literacy, just to be sure. Alas, even then, the spoken word would remain, so we might as well get to the heart of the problem; knowledge. Knowledge causes global warming.

But it is human reason that discovers knowledge, creativity that applies it, love that impels its application, and freedom that allows reason, love, and creativity to act. So then, if we are really committed to the protection of climatic stasis, reason must be suppressed, creativity placed in chains, love abandoned, and freedom abolished. To do otherwise is to risk the fate of the Earth. Vice, on the other hand, is to be celebrated. For it is those who steal their wealth, rather than those who produce it, who have minimal environmental impact; and those who harm others, who limit their human potential, constrain their aspirations, and who cut short their hopes, their dreams, and their lives, who are the true heroes of the new creed.

Thus envirostasis thought turns morality on its head. Anything good becomes evil, and all evil becomes good. Searchinger condemns the US corn ethanol program because it allegedly opens up market opportunities for third world peasants. It doesn't—so factually he is wrong—but that is not the problem. *The problem is that his paper opposes the program precisely because of the humanitarian good that it might do.*

So the critical issue at stake ultimately is not ethanol; it's ethics. In their ongoing discourse, Left and Right have frequently disagreed on what policies might best advance human well-being, but nevertheless agreed that the advance of human welfare should be the goal of policy. So, for example, the Left might say that minimum wage laws are good for the human condition because they raise the income levels of the poor, while the Right might say they are bad because they cause unemployment; but each side can still break bread with the other, because they both represent rational attempts to reach a common end by alternate means. Republicans might look askance at the universal health care plans currently being offered by the Democrats, but certainly no one can object to the goal of improving health care or making it more affordable. Left and Right might disagree on whether public schools or vouchers provide the best educational system, but they both concur that the best educational system should be the goal.

At least that's how it's been up till now. However, if generally accepted, envirostasis ideology provides a radically different way of addressing such problems. Instead of seeking to raise incomes or employment among the poor, we should seek to depress both. Instead of trying to make our health care system more effective or affordable, we should do the opposite. Instead of trying to create the best educational system, we should strive for the worst.

And thus we see the ethic of envirostasis revealed for what it really is: rank Malthusian ideology. Conservatives should oppose it for its deeply degrading anti-humanism. And liberals, too, should be wary of making common cause with it for the sake of its concern about the environment, because all of the proudest accomplishments of both modern and historical liberalism—child labor laws, minimum wage laws, public schools, libraries, urban sanitation, childhood vaccinations, public health services, rural electrification, transportation infrastructure, social security, clean air and water laws, civil rights laws, and even African-American emancipation, popular enfranchisement, representative government, and independence from colonial rule—all indirectly contribute to carbon emissions, and thus must be ultimately rejected by the cult of envirostasis.

The Real Ethanol Issue

Global warming is real. According to well-substantiated measurements, average worldwide temperatures have been increasing for the past several decades at a rate of 0.2 degrees Celsius per decade—a rate that if left unchecked for another century would bring temperatures back where they were 1,000 years ago, and might raise sea levels approximately one foot. Such a moderate change would hardly be a major threat, and could even be beneficial—as it clearly was during the High Middle Ages.

However, there is solid reason to believe that this temperature rise is being driven by human carbon dioxide emissions, which are rising as the global economy expands. We will thus need to eventually get carbon dioxide emissions under control. If done properly, replacing petroleum-derived fuels with biofuels can be of great assistance in doing so, and the evidence suggests that corn ethanol already is making a contribution in that direction.

There is a real flaw in the US corn ethanol program, however, and that is its size: it is much too *small* to effectively address the pressing problem of the looting of our economy by the oil cartel. To put the matter simply, it's not about the weather; it's about the money. The ethanol program is now demonstrably cutting the nation's tribute to the oil cartel by tens of billions of dollars per year. But we need to do much more. When 2008 oil prices return, as they surely will if the economy begins to recover, the United States will again pay $600 billion or more for oil imports each year, an amount coming *out* of the US economy that is comparable to the budget busting emergency stimulus that Congress threw *into* our economy to stave off depression. Under these circumstances, our nation's modest biofuels program just isn't enough.

We need to do more—and can. Congress should take the critical step required to break OPEC's vertical monopoly on our economic lifeblood by passing a bill mandating that all new cars sold in the United States be flexible-fueled—that is, able to run on any combination of gasoline, ethanol, or methanol. Such cars already exist and only cost about $100 more than comparable non-flex-fuel models. By making flex-fuel a requirement for the American auto market, we will make it the international standard as well, and will for the first time force gasoline to compete at the pump against alcohol fuels all over the world.

Such a flex fuel vehicle standard would create a global open source fuel market that would encourage the rise of not only existing sugar and corn ethanol, but of other alcohols as well, including ethanol made from cellulosic material, and methanol, which can be made from any kind of biomass without exception (as well as from coal, natural gas, and even recycled urban trash). By making our cars compatible with such fuels, we will enormously expand and diversify our options, protecting not just Americans but the entire world from domination by the oil cartel.

So long as we do not have fuel choice, the nation will remain at the mercy of the oil cartel, forced to pay any tribute they dictate—whether $100/barrel next year or $200/barrel the year after—giving trillions of dollars to Islamists to promote global jihad, fund nuclear weapons development, and take over our corporations and media organizations. But once we open the fuel market, we will put a permanent constraint on the greed and power of our enemies. Indeed, once we have an alternative fuel infrastructure in place, we can defeat them utterly at our pleasure by systematically implementing tax and tariff policies that favor alcohols over oil.

And yes, under those conditions, we will actually create markets for ethanol derived from third world farm products, opening up income opportunities for billions of poor people around the world—just what the envirostasists fear most. We will, in effect, redirect hundreds of billions of dollars from the oil cartel to the world's agricultural sector, creating an enormous engine for global development that will lift whole nations out of poverty.

That will be a very *good* thing to do, and by choosing such a course of action, we will reaffirm human progress as the ethical basis of our society. It will also deliver a powerful rebuke to both the Malthusians and Islamists, whose common program is not only high oil prices, but the stifling of human initiative and the crushing of human aspirations in order to preserve stasis.

This, and not retreat from the small but promising start the corn ethanol program has made, should be our course. We should not be deterred from it by Malthusian quackery masquerading as science. ﹀

References

1. Muriel Boselli, "Saudi oil minister slams biofuels, supports solar energy," Reuters, April 10, 2008, http://uk.reuters.com/article/environmentNews/idUKL1079284820080410

2. "OPEC president blames ethanol for crude-price rise," MarketWatch, July 6, 2008, http://www.marketwatch.com/news/story/opec-president-blames-oil-prices/story.aspx?guid=%7BE003D4C9-0739-4868-8F69-D9C51BB53CB5%7D

3. "Chavez calls ethanol production 'crime'," Associated Press, April 26, 2008, http://www.newsmax.com/international/venezuela_ethanol/2008/04/26/91282.html

4. "Report of the Attorney General to the Congress of the United States on the Administration of the Foreign Agents Registration Act of 1938, as amended, for the first six months ending June 30 2007," US Department of Justice, Washington DC, http://www.usdoj.gov/criminal/fara/reports/June30-2007.pdf

5. Anna Palmer, "Beating up on Ethanol," *Roll Call*, May 14, 2008, http://www.rollcall.com/issues/53_137/news/23620-1.html?type=printer_friendly

6. Timothy Searchinger *et al.*, "Use of US Croplands for Biofuels Increases Greenhouse Gases Through Emissions from Land-Use Change," Science vol 319, 29 February 2008, pp. 1238-1240, subsequently circulated in more readable form by Searchinger alone in a policy paper issued by the German Marshall Fund.

7. Michael Wang and Zia Haq, "Letter to Science," February 14, 2008, revised March 14, 2008, http://www.transportation.anl.gov/pdfs/letter_to_science_anldoe_03_14_08.pdf

The World According to Biofuels

WESLEY K. CLARK

A merican troops in the Middle East? In the Persian Gulf? To secure access to oil? Highly unlikely, would never happen, my bosses in the Pentagon told me as I briefed my analysis of the newest national security issue: energy. It was the summer of 1973, and as an Army Captain teaching at West Point, I had a summer assignment to study the energy crisis and its implications for national security. Our nation was in the aftermath of Vietnam. The POWs had just returned home, and the Army was gunshy about predicting to Congress

During thirty-four years of service in the United States Army, Wesley K. Clark rose to the rank of four-star general as NATO's Supreme Allied Commander, Europe. After his retirement in 2000, he became an investment banker, author, commentator, and businessman. He is the author of *Waging Modern War: Bosnia, Kosovo and the Future of* Combat (Public Affairs, 2001) and *Winning Modern War: Iraq, Terrorism and the American Empire* (Public Affairs, 2003).

or even its own superiors inside the Pentagon how it might, in the future, be called to serve.

Nevertheless, I prepared and submitted my analysis, however skeptical the audience. It was about our growing dependence on imported oil, I explained. We would have to eventually take measures to assure our access to our economic lifeblood. Now, however, some 37 years later, the "unlikely" is the nightmare we have been living with for almost twenty years. The truth is that the US is an oil-importing nation; and step-by-step, we have been drawn into the

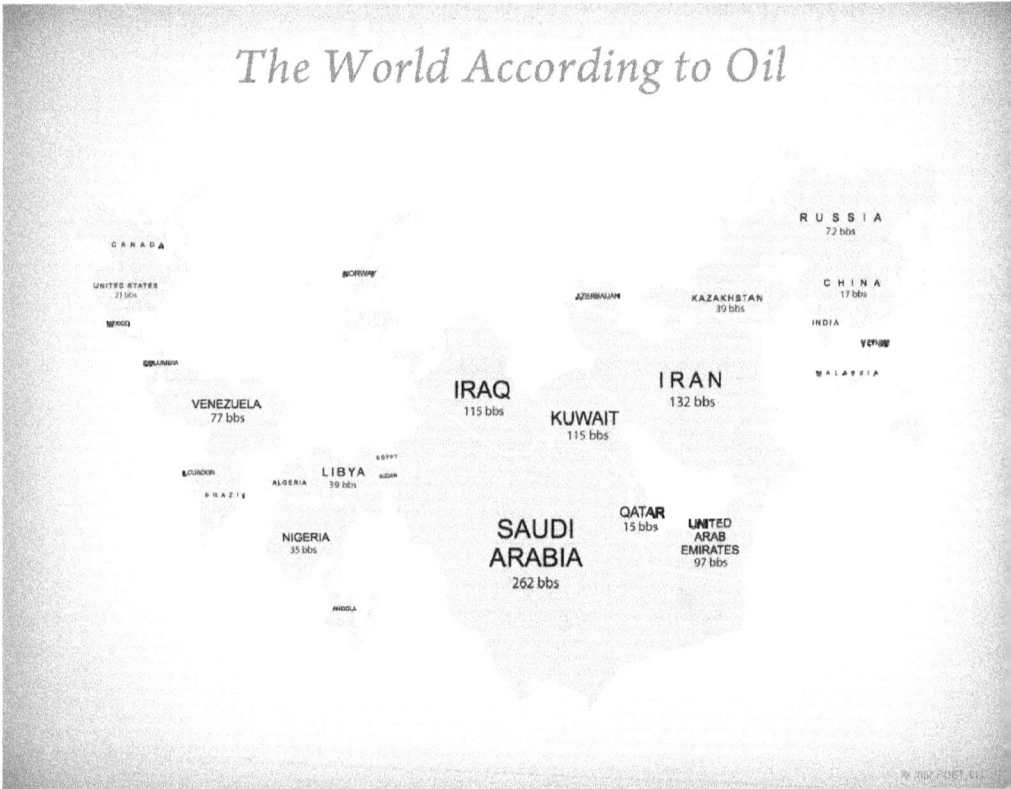

The World According to Oil

RUSSIA
72 bbs

CANADA

UNITED STATES
21 bbs

NORWAY

CHINA
17 bbs

AZERBAIJAN

KAZAKHSTAN
39 bbs

INDIA

MEXICO

VIETNAM

COLUMBIA

MALAYSIA

VENEZUELA
77 bbs

IRAQ
115 bbs

IRAN
132 bbs

KUWAIT
115 bbs

ECUADOR

EGYPT

LIBYA
39 bbs

ALGERIA

SUDAN

BRAZIL

NIGERIA
35 bbs

SAUDI
ARABIA
262 bbs

QATAR
15 bbs

UNITED
ARAB
EMIRATES
97 bbs

ANGOLA

Source: Growth Energy. *This chart is based on information from BP Statistical Review Year End 2004 and from the Energy Information Administration.*

Mideast in a way that has proved incredibly costly to the nation and to our own armed forces.

As early as the late 70's the Pentagon recognized its error. A Rapid Deployment Joint Task Force targeted on intervention in the Gulf was established. In the early 1980's, the US Central Command was formed; then the US Fifth Fleet was formed. In the late 1980's we engaged Iran in the so-called "tanker war," escorting oil tankers in the face of Iranian threats. In 1990, in response to the Iraqi invasion and occupation of Kuwait, we launched Operation Desert Shield, and deployed several hundred thousand troops, ships and aircraft to the region. And in mid-January, 1991, we went to war with Iraq. It was, in the words of then Secretary of State Jim Baker, "about oil."

Thirty-seven years later, over the course of six presidencies, we still have an energy policy that keeps us inexorably linked to regions of the world that are unstable and, on occasion, hostile to our interests as a nation. And we are paying a very heavy price. Beyond the cost in lives and treasure, our foreign policy has become distorted in the competition for energy resources. We created a whole new class of international financial assets—petrodollars—which have funded many nations whose interests were antithetical to our own, and others so plagued by corruption and mismanagement that the resources they received actually destroyed their opportunities for development. And for the United States itself, in a scenario where oil costs $70-$80 dollars per barrel, we are giving out the largest booty in the history of civilization, transferring annually between $250 to $400 billion dollars from our own economy to oil exporting nations. That works out to a "tax" on Americans of some $1,000 per year for every man woman and child in this country. It saps American job creation, and weighs heavily on our future economic growth. It is a tragedy of historic proportions.

The US Department of Energy found that America's dependence on foreign oil has cost our country more than $7 trillion dollars over the last 30 years.

That is an enormous amount of money to transfer out of our economy. Think of what we could do in our nation with just a fraction of that money reinvested in our rural communities, our schools, our hospitals and research centers. Think of how secure we would be as a nation if we refused to send that money overseas, where so much of it ends up funding anti-American activities, including the evil work of terrorist organizations.

It is wrong, and it should change.

Reducing America's dependence on foreign oil goes hand-in-hand with keeping our country safe, and protecting our economic security. The simple fact is that our national security is diminished with every barrel of imported oil we consume.

There is an Alternative: Domestic Ethanol

It doesn't have to be this way. We have alternative sources to foreign oil that are sustainable, renewable—and best of all—domestic. The best alternative to gasoline refined from foreign oil is ethanol. Ethanol is one of our earliest fuels in this country; the original Model T was fueled on ethanol, and even then Henry Ford knew of ethanol's potential when he told a New York Times reporter in 1925 that ethanol could be made out of any number of feedstock. Ford singled out sumach, weeds and sawdust.

Ethanol is not a "some day" answer to our nation's energy crisis; eight out of every 10 gallons of gasoline sold in the United States has some ethanol already blended into it. It is not dependent on a technology that has yet to be developed, and it would not require a massive shift in the driving and fueling habits of American consumers. Ethanol creates US jobs, and grain ethanol is 59 percent cleaner than gasoline, according to a study published by the Yale's Journal of Industrial Ecology. Ethanol—particularly grain ethanol—has the potential to play a much greater role in reducing our dependence on foreign oil. And it should.

Today most of the ethanol made in the United States is corn ethanol. Grain ethanol is one of the cheapest, most abundant sources of alternative fuel available in our country. And as a nation, we are on track to produce enough grain and cellulosic ethanol in this country to substantially reduce the amount of oil we would need to import—and possibly end petroleum's dominance over our economy.

We Have the Capacity to Produce Enough
Ethanol to Make a Difference

The domestic production of nearly 9 billion gallons of ethanol in 2008 eliminated the need to import at least 321.4 million barrels of oil to manufacture gasoline—roughly five percent of US crude imports.

The World According to Agriculture

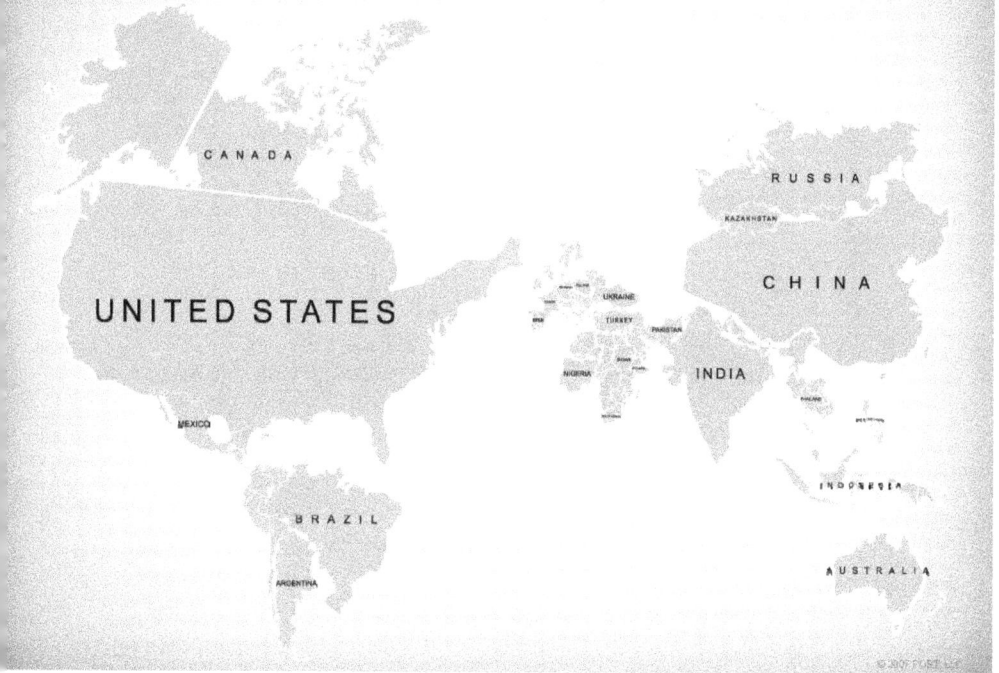

CANADA

RUSSIA

KAZAKHSTAN

UNITED STATES

CHINA

UKRAINE

TURKEY

PAKISTAN

NIGERIA

INDIA

MEXICO

INDONESIA

BRAZIL

AUSTRALIA

ARGENTINA

Source: Growth Energy. *This chart is based on information from the USDA 2009/2010 Production as of January 2010 Crop Report.*

The commercialization of cellulosic ethanol offers even greater potential to further US energy independence. According to a recent Sandia National Laboratory and General Motors report, biofuels could replace nearly a third of current US gasoline use by the year 2030.

Opponents of ethanol mistakenly claim that we cannot produce enough grain in the United States to meet our needs for food, fuel and livestock feed. In fact we can, and have been.

One hundred years ago, the average yield for corn per acre was 27.9 bushels. Fifty years ago it rose to 54.7 bushels per acre. In 2000, yield rose to 136.9 bushels per acre. And this last year, American farmers produced an all-time corn crop with an average yield of more than 165 bushels per acre.

And this 13 billion bushel record was produced on 7 million fewer acres than the previous record crop in this country, set in 2007. We are also increasing the amount of energy we can draw from each bushel. Today we are generating about 3 gallons of ethanol out of each bushel, up from 2.5 gallons nearly 20 years ago.

Efficiencies, innovation and technological advancements in farming and ethanol production will continue to push up grain yields—producing more than enough grain to meet our domestic needs—and the amount of ethanol we can produce out of each bushel.

Our agricultural potential as a country is one of our greatest assets. We should be deploying this asset to strengthen our national and economic defenses, and reduce our dependence on imported oil, by producing more domestic ethanol. Considering the global race to develop green technology, the US would be making a grave mistake to not pursue further development in agricultural innovation and biofuel industries.

Right now the US is a world leader in agriculture production. In 2008, China produced 87.3 bushels of corn per acre, and Brazil produced only 60 bushels per acre. If those two countries produced 25 percent more—an improvement which would still leave their yields significantly below US yields—it would add 2.1 billion bushels of corn annually to the world market. That is more than current US exports, and it is easily possible if either of those countries adopted technology and practices that are common today in the United States.

Maintaining our nation's advantage in this area means developing cellulosic ethanol, which will bring more efficiency improvements and a drastic expansion in the types of available feedstock. Cellulosic ethanol is a 50-state renewable fuel solution: it can be derived from citrus pulp in Florida, woodchips in Vermont, shredded paper in New Jersey, or municipal solid waste in California.

The Sandia National Laboratory and General Motors Corp. study concluded that with development of technology and feedstocks, cellulosic ethanol could compete without incentives by 2030 when oil is priced between $70 and $90 per barrel. As an emerging competitor to a well-entrenched, global petroleum industry, cellulosic ethanol's positive characteristics—from domestic job creation to reduced greenhouse gas emissions, on top of national security issues—demand that we provide sound public policy to support the rapid development of cellulosic fuel technology.

A Fuel Technology That Could Stabilize
Troubled Nations—and Reduce Threats

C ellulose is the most common renewable biomass on the planet. It is found in all plants.

The technology of cellulosic ethanol means that we could produce ethanol in every state in the nation. But taking that idea a step farther, the technology of cellulosic ethanol could be used all over the world to help make developing nations energy in-dependent—breaking the yoke of strongmen, rogue nations and cartel-driven energy prices not just on our economy, but on the economies of those nations that are most vulnerable.

Here the United States can invest in developing countries—helping those growing economies create their own domestic, re-newable fuel industries—as part of a strategy to bolster our own economic and national security. Instead of sending soldiers into some of these countries to find terrorists and their training camps, we could be sending in American technology and investment in something that every country needs: a domestic source of renew-able transportation fuel.

The United States can find national security by changing the conditions in which so many around the world live. With the devel-opment of economic tools, like renewable ethanol industries, poorer countries could begin to enjoy the fruits of a modern world—better schools, better health care, and better jobs—that we enjoy here in the United States.

Domestic Production Must Increase by Lifting
Regulatory Caps

T here are many hurdles that lie before us to increase the pro-duction of domestic ethanol. We need to expand the market opportunity for ethanol production and consumption to reach that significant potential. That starts by increasing the federal government's arbitrary cap on the amount of ethanol blended into gasoline from the current level of 10 percent. Growth Energy led an initiative to petition the federal government to lift that regulatory cap on ethanol's market.

In December, the US Environmental Protection Agency (EPA) took an important first step toward accomplishing this when it issued a letter stating that testing of engine, fuel and emissions systems on today's generation of automobiles shows they are sufficiently durable to use gasoline blended with as much as 15 percent ethanol.

While a final decision by the EPA is pending, EPA Administrator Lisa Jackson has indicated that newer vehicles will likely be able to accommodate E15 blends—a strong signal that the US is preparing to move to E15 and a renewed commitment to increase the use of homegrown, domestic fuels.

While this may not seem like much—a change of only 5 percent in the overall fuel mix—it would have enormous ramifications, all of which are positive. Such a move will disrupt the importation of seven billion gallons of foreign oil each year, create as many as 136,000 permanent jobs in the US, and substantially green the environment. It also fulfills a pledge that President Obama made at the onset of his Administration to base public policies on the soundest of science.

Let there be no doubt on this point. An overwhelming body of sound science supports the use of more ethanol, such as E15, in the majority of vehicles on the road today. There has been more testing of E15 than any other fuel additive in the history of the EPA waiver process. Multiple studies by government agencies and academic institutions all point to the same thing: E15 has no adverse impact on an engine's performance, maintenance or emissions, yet expands consumer choice and improves the economic and national security of our country.

There are other positive signs for American ethanol and other biofuels. President Obama issued the first report by his Interagency Biofuels Working Group, outlining his Administration's goals to boost the amount of ethanol and other biofuels produced and consumed in the United States.

In February, EPA issued its newly-expanded Renewable Fuels Standard, based on the 2007 Energy Independence and Security Act passed by Congress. The new RFS found that grain ethanol meets the definition of being a low-carbon fuel, even when incorporating highly-controversial and scientifically-unsettled penalties based on so-called "indirect land use change" theories that would charge American producers for the carbon released by farmers half a world away. The EPA found that, despite the ILUC penalties, corn ethanol is at least 20 percent cleaner than gasoline.

All these moves by the Obama Administration and Congress show that our policymakers know there is a problem with our nation's addiction to foreign oil: the risks range from cartel-driven oil shocks to our economy, to the fact that by sending our money overseas to we are underwriting the very terrorists who seek to dismantle American society.

If we are to fulfill our national aspiration to be energy independent, if we are to improve American security by lessening our global risks and build a stronger and more vibrant economy at home, we must urge our leaders to continue to advance policies that will further the availability and use of homegrown, renewable fuels.

We have a chance to do that. After 37 years, it is long past time. [1]

Is the War Over Oil?

BURL HAIGWOOD

A key issue confronting policymakers is how to communicate with ordinary people about the issue of energy security. This article provides a baseline of validated public information layered with context and perspectives about energy security, the path and roadblocks to alternative fuels, and the impact of oil use on the individual's economic, environmental, and national security.

It is up to each individual to decide which way their moral compass is pointing and determine why they may or may not be treating the development of alternatives to crude

Burl Haigwood is the Director of Program Development for the Clean Fuels Development Coalition (CFDC). He has held positions in the corporate and non-profit sectors and supported the organizational development of the Renewable Fuels Association, the Clean Fuels Development Coalition, and the Clean Fuels Foundation. From 1999-2006 Mr. Haigwood was the Manager of Consulting Services for Oracle supporting the Environmental Protection Agency and Department of Energy.

oil use with the same importance, unquestioned reverence, and sense of urgency as national security.

Energy policy has forced the United States into a problematic long-term national security strategy to protect the supply, transportation, and artificially low price of crude oil. Perhaps that is why many in government and industry still refuse to talk openly about the billion-dollar-a-day fossil-fueled dinosaur metaphorically sitting in the war room at the Pentagon. Further still, the consumption habits of the average US consumer have in fact caused the "War-Over-Oil." What is clear, however, is that the spoils of victory, or the cost of defeat, will surely include geopolitical and economic stability for generations to come.

The quest for energy/national security is not altruistic: the oil business has become very personal. Energy security is synonymous with national security. National security is synonymous with personal security. Very few analytical avenues would not a lead a person seeking an explanation of energy security to a road paved with oil and full of economic, environmental, and national security potholes. The road to energy/national security intersects at imported oil and has a gasoline station on each corner.

Not all forms of alternative energy are equal when it comes to energy/national security. Less than 5% of world's oil is used to generate electricity. *Making clean electricity is important to our environment and economy, but solar, wind, geothermal and even natural gas do almost nothing to curb or stop oil imports.* The US energy/national security focus should be about oil in general, imported oil specifically, and about replacing gasoline—emphatically.

Why the sense of urgency? If the US made every new car electric or natural gas fueled and consumers bought them, it would take 17 years to replace the 230 million cars on the road that are 100% dependent on gasoline. Even the fuel-efficient hybrids in show rooms today will be 100% dependent on gasoline for the next 17 years!

The following quotations do not need much interpretation. These experts have access to critical information needed to make informed decisions about the US energy/national security situation --information that most people do not have the security clearances to see. Leaders of the Republican and Democratic parties have reached a consensus that the fine line between energy security and national security is hardwired and the goal of enhancing national security is extremely urgent.

We are reaching a point of absolute consensus that we need to take control of our energy future… This is not about Republicans or Democrats, federal government or state government, but instead it is a government for the entire nation.—*US Senator Ben Nelson (D-NE) September 2007.*

We simply must diversify our sources of energy, and we must do so in a way that lessens our dependence on foreign sources for this energy. The fact that almost 60% of our energy sources are coming from overseas is simply too much, it is unacceptable today. America's energy policy should be consistent with our foreign policy in that it has the principles of independence and security at its foundation. —*US Senator Bill Frist (R-TN), July 2003.*

The Governors' Ethanol Coalition, which represents 30 Governors [36 today], believes that increasing dependence on foreign oil is a major risk to the nation's energy, economic, and environmental security. —*Governors' Ethanol Coalition letter to President George W. Bush, April 2005.*

To safeguard our future economic health as well as our national security, we must move aggressively to diversify our energy sources. Every time we visit the gas pump these days, we are reminded that there is no time to waste. —*Samuel W. Bodman, Secretary of Energy, July 2006.*

From all of the quotations it appears that the public and politicians have reached consensus! Political consensus is a powerful message and an absolute warning to the public that the nation's oil addiction has reached a point where intervention is a necessity.

However, what about the opinions of leaders of the Army, Navy, Marines, Air Force, Central Intelligence Agency, Department of Energy, and top Fortune 50 companies? These are also experts in the field of energy security. These experts literally fight everyday for your energy and economic freedoms and they certainly understand and agree that the line between energy policy and national security is blurring.

In the interests of our national security, our climate, and our pocket books, we should now move together as a nation – indeed as a community of oil importer nations – to destroy, not oil of course, but oil's strategic role in transportation as quickly and as thoroughly as possible. The national security reasons to destroy oil's strategic role are substantial.

Over two-thirds of the world's proven reserves of conventional oil lie in the turbulent states of the Persian Gulf, as does much of the oil's international infrastructure. Increasing dependence on this part of the world for our transportation needs is subject to a wide range of perils. Just over a year ago, in response to bin Laden's many calls for attack on such infrastructure, al Qaeda attacked Abcaiq, the world's largest oil production facility, in northeastern Saudi Arabia. Had it succeeded in destroying, e.g., the sulfur-clearing towers there through which about two-thirds of Saudi crude passes – say with a simple mortar attack – it would have succeeded in driving the price of oil to over $100 per barrel for many months, perhaps close to bin Laden's goal of $200 per barrel. What we need is a transportation fuel that is as secure as possible, as clean as possible and as cheap as possible. Today, oil meets none of these needs. —*Former CIA Director James Woolsey before the Senate Finance Committee, April 2007*

A new study ordered by the Pentagon warns that the rising cost and dwindling supply of oil—the lifeblood of fighter jets, warships, and tanks—will make the US military's ability to respond to hot spots around the world 'unsustainable in the long term.' The costs of relying on oil to power the military are consuming an increasing share of the military's budget. Energy costs have doubled since the terrorist attacks of Sept. 11, 2001, and the cost of conducting operations could become so expensive in the future that the military will not be able to pay for some of its new weapon systems. All four branches of the military must 'fundamentally transform' their assumptions about energy, including taking immediate steps toward fielding weapons systems and aircraft that run on alternative and renewable fuels. — *The Boston Globe, May 2007*

We need an energy policy in this country that helps break our dependence on oil imported from countries that don't share American interests, and we have an enormous opportunity to do that with ethanol. Within four years, we can replace the importation of more than one million barrels of oil per day with domestic ethanol. That would take Hugo Chavez out of the US energy market.—*Gen. Wesley Clark (Ret.)*

The intent of this article is not to advocate that the US should, could, can, or will remove itself from present *War- Over-Oil;* it is to question our national progress on developing alternatives to oil use and to recognize our moral responsibility to face the consequences of long-term conflicts over oil. The intent is also to create an assessment tool to help people (1) understand who has the authority and responsibility for change; (2) recognize the consequences of failure; and (3) appreciate the degree of difficulty involved in convincing US policy makers to break through the alternative fuel roadblocks.

This is also not an attempt to throw any non-oil choice under the alternative fuel bus. Change will take everything the United States and its allies have in their oil reduction arsenals. These facts and opinions are provided with the intent to encourage people not to take "the-alternative-fuels-world-is-flat" bait or the "alternative-fuels-are-bad" hook being fished in the media by representatives of companies competing for the world's largest gasoline market. Ethanol and biofuels are often used as examples in this article because ethanol is the only commercially available alternative to gasoline in the market place today. Ethanol is not necessarily preferred or perfect, but it does replace oil. Moreover, it therefore provides a learning opportunity and platform for market-based comparisons to other alternative fuels.

In the pages that follow, we lay out a sequence of the various perspectives from which the informed layperson might approach energy security: as a researcher, as an analyst, and finally as a political leader. The essay employs "you" in the second person to address this audience directly.

I hope this essay provides useful approaches to those of us who, in our capacities as policymakers, academics, or public educators, have as our everyday mission the responsibility of reaching out to the public on energy security in one way or another.

To the Researcher

Research involves compiling historical facts about an issue. What are historical precedents? There are ten basic facts about the world oil supply that greatly contribute to the US capability to define our national security and energy security goals. Predictions regarding the location, ownership, and future demand on the world's oil supply by the United States, indicate a diminishing US capability to live up to its democratic and capitalistic principles. In fact, these facts and predictions indicate that current energy policy is jeopardizing the US's ability to present consistent policies concerning democratic and capitalistic ideas to both oil-producing and non-oil-producing countries. These facts are as follows:

The International Energy Agency (IEA) projects world oil demand to double by 2030. The red portion of the bar on the chart to the right illustrates the additional 50 million barrels per day of oil EIA has classified as "yet to be developed or found." The yet to be found supply is the equivalent of finding the equivalent of two new fields similar in size to those in Saudi Arabia—the world's largest producer of oil. The US consumes 25% of the world's oil and geographically has only 3% of its proven reserves. Long lasting economic downturn has persistently followed every spike in oil price. Countries, not companies own about 80% of the world's oil. Foreign governments own the top ten oil and natural gas companies. All US oil companies *combined* control less than 10% of the world's oil reserves. Exxon Mobil – the largest US oil company is *not* among the top 10 largest oil reserve holders. As a result, the US imports 60% of its oil and that is expected to increase to 70% by 2030.

Nearly 70% of all of the proven oil reserves in the world are located in the Middle East. The Organization of Petroleum Exporting Countries (OPEC) own 78% of the world oil supply and 40% of the world oil-import market.

A generation ago, the reliance on US military power was codified in the 1980 Carter Doctrine, a vow by the US to defend Persian Gulf oil from the Soviets. President Reagan put the doctrine into practice by creating an American military command in the Gulf, and later ordering the Navy to protect Kuwaiti oil tankers during the Iran-Iraq War of the 1980s. In the mid 1980's the Middle East became the Central Command's top priority. The portion of the US military activity and budget focused on the Middle East has been growing larger for the past twenty years.

Saddam Hussein publically stated he invaded Kuwait in the hopes of controlling the supplies and prices of crude oil in the Middle East. His decision to burn the oil fields was a clear indication of his intent to harm the US and world economies using oil as a weapon of mass economic destruction. This was not the first or last time oil has been used as a weapon against the US.

The al-Qaeda network is constantly testing the relationship between the US and the world's largest oil producer, Saudi Arabia and other oil producers. It is an established fact that many terrorists groups' goals include destroying the ability of Saudi Arabia and others to produce oil/gasoline for the world market.

Oil producing regions in West Africa and the Caspian Sea are becoming targets for terrorists and dictatorships that do not have the stability of the world's economy as one of their vested interests.

> Vital economic interests are at risk as well. Iraq itself controls some 10 percent of the world's proven oil reserves. Iraq plus Kuwait controls twice that. An Iraq permitted to swallow Kuwait would have the economic and military power, as well as the arrogance, to intimidate and coerce its neighbors—neighbors who control the lion's share of the world's remaining oil reserves. We cannot permit a resource so vital to be dominated by one so ruthless. And we won't. —*President George H. W. Bush, September 11, 1990, Address Before a Joint Session of Congress.*

However, the idea of using the oil as a weapon or oil embargoes for geopolitical messages to alter other states' foreign policy was not new in 1973. In August 1941, when the United States was in control of a relatively much larger percentage of the world oil supply, the US supplied Japan with an estimated 80-93% of its oil supply. President Roosevelt placed an oil embargo on Japan following the Japanese invasion of Indochina in 1940. It caused an economic crisis in Japan ultimately causing the Japanese to further their war efforts to obtain control of the oil-rich Dutch East Indies. Their decision to attack Pearl Harbor was the first, but not the last, attack on US soil related to oil. The War in the Pacific, Japan's war over oil started with an oil embargo, included the oft-forgotten Japanese shelling of a Santa Barbara oil refinery, and ended with two atomic mushroom clouds.

Since the first oil embargo against the United States in 1973, US gasoline demand has increased by 40 billion gallons. In spite of warnings, wars, and record profits, major oil companies and/or the DOD and its research agencies have yet to integrate the use of a commercially available alternative fuel into the energy and national security agenda. Many can understand the decision of the major oil companies to continue the drive to secure oil, by why the DOD? When considering DOD is the world's largest consumer of oil, it would appear logical they would want to keep oil prices low, but should they not also encourage the public to use alternative fuels and to safeguard American soldiers by strategically devaluing the need for the oil they are fighting to protect.

To the Analyst

There are questions that concerned analysts should ask themselves regarding the outcome of contemporary oil-related conflicts. These are as follows:

If 70% of proven oil reserves were not located in the Middle East, would the region still be of strategic concern?

If Saddam Hussein did not have the enormous revenues from oil exports could he have purchased the military equipment needed to invade Iran or Kuwait?

Would Iran be pursuing nuclear arms without the luxury of years of crude oil revenue from its oil exports? Is their nuclear program really aimed at providing electricity? Is their pursuit of nuclear energy a signal their oil production is slowing, or is hiding their nuclear research in a bunker on the side of a mountain a better indication of their intentions?

Consider that other nation-states and non-government actors are aware of the US's dependency on foreign oil and the US's overall economic vulnerability due to the decreased domestic production of an array of natural resources. Is a thorough analysis of these vulnerabilities necessary before we can correct the obvious flaws in our current energy policy? If a foreign actor were to declare war on the US, would it be strategically favorable for them to use oil as a weapon? What other energy networks are vulnerable?

If people still think oil is not our top energy/national security problem, they should consider the US Petroleum Production Capacity and Demand chart, illustrating our national demand, production, and oil import data. Note the trends after the US reached "peak oil" production in 1970. Most would agree that the quality of US energy/national security has declined in the past 30 years.

To the Policymaker

The policymaker's job is to enact laws and policies that provide incentives and disincentives to change the behaviors of both the consumer and *government*. These laws ought to be designed to further the national security interests of the country and still allow for market freedom. Creating these policies will have the affect of securing the US's ability to maintain superior armed forces and provide a profitable alternative fuel for the American consumer.

Simply put, using the military to secure the market for oil as a national deadweight loss. Thus, the solution to alternatives to oil is similar to solving an economic and security Rubik's Cube puzzle—as the functioning of all of our other markets are dependent on energy.

The alternative fuels Rubik's Cube exercise will help determine what can be done to enhance the energy/national security of the United States. Its purpose is to help the policymaker get a better understanding of alternative fuel choices as well as implement their use in a way that allows for commercial success. The purpose of the exercise is to determine what "pieces" of the puzzle need to be solved, and what policies will result in a perfectly color-coded six-sided Rubik Cube. To solve a Rubik's Cube, six colors have to be aligned to six different sides. In the case of policy, these will be "drivers." They are the underlying facts. To solve the puzzle, one has to twist and turn the different layers of the cube, horizontally and vertically realigning the cube by rows and columns. These are actions. In the case of the policy maker, the laws and precedents that can create the incentives to change behavior. To solve the puzzle of developing commercial alternatives—other than biofuels—it is necessary to identify that the puzzle pieces are. The drivers are of course: the market, cost, and national security advantage; the action realigning the pieces; policies, and the solved puzzle; a successful energy policy agenda. Below is a list of "drivers," or the puzzle pieces to be considered:

- speed-to-market
- market price of the alternative fuel
- market price of the alternative fuel vehicle
- availability of the alternative fuel and vehicle
- ability to scale up production of alternative fuels and vehicles
- speed to reach full acceptance by consumers and auto manufacturers
- time to reach and sustain brand loyalty
- cost/time/risk to convert public refueling stations
- cost/time/risk to convert the existing fleet of 230 million legacy vehicles
- diversity and availability of feedstock available to produce alternative fuels
- ability to produce the alternative fuel in a decentralized manner so it doesn't become a targets for terrorists

- total cost to the government/taxpayer
- total cost to the consumer, and the
- cost of not taking action.

These are all critical puzzle pieces that need policy solutions to result in a completed Rubik's cube; a cohesive energy/national security policy that includes a viable and sustainable substitute for gasoline. The next section is a further description of these drivers, along with facts about past twists and turns of the Rubik's Cube puzzle in the form of past policies. Each section concludes with a policy question, to put you the reader in the policy maker driver's seat and help you understand how ethanol/biofuels have emerged as the leading substitute for imported oil/gasoline.

Fueling 230 million legacy vehicles

Cash for clunkers was an interesting start at removing low mileage vehicles in the existing passenger fleet (i.e., legacy vehicles). However the incentives did not include alternative fuel vehicles, because of the small scale of production—with Flex Fuel Vehicles (FFVs) being the exception. There is one Honda natural gas vehicle, but there are no electric, LPG, hydrogen, or propane vehicles for sale. Hybrids are available but are still 100% dependent on gasoline and only save 1/10, the amount of gasoline compared to ethanol. For example, an FFV minivan fills up with 20 gallons of gasoline and goes about 400 miles, or about 20 mpg. Even considering the worst-case scenario, a 20% mileage penalty, the same minivan fills up with E85 and goes about 320 miles on 3 gallons of gasoline—or 106 miles to the gallon-of-gasoline. That is the difference between *The War-Over-Oil* and the media war over ethanol. Aside from the 8 million FFVs on the road and 36 models available in show rooms, there is little choice policy makers can focus on that will have an immediate, significant, and long-term impact on gasoline reduction—considering it takes 17 years to turn the legacy fleet over—in good economic times. History and surveys say consumers are unlikely to volunteer to convert their cars to another fuel at current gasoline prices. Should the government and taxpayers pay the difference?

Building new alternative fuel/refueling infrastructure

O ver 90% of the gasoline retail stations in the US are small independently owned businesses. Most gas station owners have balked at the offer to spend the $10,000 to $50,000 per station required to provide E85 to the 8 million FFV owners (12 million by 2012). It is highly unlikely these same small business owners will voluntarily invest the $250,000 to $1MM+ that is needed to install natural gas, LPG, hydrogen-refueling capacity, or electric– re-charging sites, especially when considering the auto-makers do not produce these cars yet or have standard batteries. Those appear to be real hurdles with a slow speed of entry into the market. On the other hand, after three years of trying, Underwriters Lab (UL) cannot seem to approve new E85 dispensers, in spite of the fact there are over 2,300 pumps already dispensing E85, 350,000 consumers using it, and every gasoline dispenser in Brazil contains at least 20% ethanol. Should the government intercede or should industry pay?

Ethanol and developing biofuels cheaper than oil

T his is a politically volatile subject, so a couple of basic facts are needed first. Ninety-eight percent of the animal feed (usually corn) grown in the Unites States is grown to feed animals—not humans. However, utilizing corn for ethanol produc-tion only removes some of the corn from animal use, as production uses only the starch portion of the feed grain with the remainder being returned to the animal feed production. Ninety six percent of the feed grain produced relies only on rain for water. The federal ethanol program has increased demand for animal feed grains and therefore animal food production in order to protect the value of farmland and keep up with increases in farmer productivity. In-creases in farmer productivity have already allowed farmers to pro-duce more feed grains (corn) than required by the Renewable Fuel Standard (RFS), on less land, with less fertilizer.

Overall, should our government and industry leaders bend to the political pressure created in the media from biofuel detractors claiming the moral issue of food vs. fuel? Will their courage and leadership allow their moral compass to point towards ethanol or more wars-over-oil? The US has over 1 billion tons of cellulose available to produce these fuels—it would cost nearly $2.30 per gallon to produce – about 50 to 75 cents more than cow-feed-based ethanol. Considering the economic, environmental, and national security payouts, that is NOT too much to pay for energy security. Detractors must consider war, loss of jobs, and $4 at the pump to be much more effective and longer-term strategies to reduce the gasoline consumption for the next generation of drivers—when compared to biofuels.

Considering we are already experiencing conflicts over vitally strategic oil, is a 10% to 20% increase in gasoline prices reasonable? This price has been proven to lower gasoline consumption by 10%. Is that too much to ask the consumer? The rationale behind the cost: ethanol blends of 40% to 85% can reduce mileage by 10-20%, but they reduce the use of gasoline consumption by 40% to 85%. Considering the consequences—which does not include a significant cost, but still leads to the creation of competition, jobs, economic stimulation—this should be a direct incentive to produce biofuels. Consumers have already shown they are willing to pay 1,000% more for spring water, Starbucks, organic food, luxury cars, and top shelf liquor—why not alternative fuels?

Here are a few more sides of the alternative fuels Rubik's Cube that need to be lined up to enhance energy/national security.

Consumer education determines viability

The oil industry is unlikely to invest capital in educating consumers on why they should buy alternative fuels. Automakers and alternative fuel makers cannot afford sustained long-term campaign, in the face of fierce and unfair competition that is already evident in the marketplace. Who is left? An inventory of those with the authority, market place responsibilities, and financial means (e.g., major oil companies, Department of Defense/DARPA) have not really encourage the use or development of commercial alternative fuel since President Carter declared the first energy crisis the "moral equivalent of war" over thirty years ago. Will an all-volunteer public education campaign drive the change needed? If alternatives are economical, will the market take care of itself?

The environmental lobby has not been helpful

I n many cases, the environmental lobby has not been supportive in developing alternative fuels. Their present demand that cellulosic and advanced biofuels be *50% to 60% better than gasoline* has become a deterrent to biofuel progress and is unreasonable, especially when considering that they would be content with a 10%-20% reduction in greenhouse gas emissions. Their efforts to disqualify the most abundant wood and agriculture waste resources by defining it as feedstock, instead of utilizing it for new ethanol technologies, is not helpful as we try to develop new non-feed grain based biofuels. Ignoring the environmental impact of oil and the consequences associated with indirect land such as war, terrorist attacks on oil installations, is disingenuous, and a disregards their ethical responsibility to show people the entire picture. Squabbling over small details of the emerging biofuels industry, in the face of an energy/national security crisis, is tantamount to arguing over the arrangement of the chairs on the deck of the Titanic. The environmental community needs to make human protection as important as environmental protection. Who will educate them?

DOD can affect policy

O verall, reducing oil use and replacing gasoline should be our nation's top energy/national security concern, and therefore a top research priority—especially for the DOD. The Department of Defense is the world's largest consumer of oil. The world oil market is fungible and fluid. Therefore, adding fuel supply to the US gasoline market via biofuels and other alternative fuels would reduce the demand pressure and price of oil being used by DOD, which can find and use crude oil supplies from all regions of the world. With a reduction in demand, it would be easier for DOD to develop technologies that would immediately replace gasoline in cars, rather than develop and replace the various types of fuels needed for tanks, ships, and aircraft. It appears that if developing alternative liquid transportation fuels (e.g., ethanol, cellulosic ethanol, advanced biofuels, biodiesel, biocrude, and everything else) becomes a priority of Congress and the DOD, there would be less pressure for the DOD to defend the entire world's oil supply, and fewer obstacles in providing oil to fuel the US Armed Forces.

What is clear from this exercise is that policymakers should create flexible policies. These policies need to be flexible enough to encourage the utilization of a diverse number of resources for energy and not encourage dependence on a single energy source- as that will lead to strategic vulnerability. What is clear is that current policy choices are analogous to removing the stickers of a Rubik's cube and then rearranging them so they are on the correct side. Our current policies are temporary fixes, that do not accomplish much, and they ultimately do not solve the puzzle, which is in this case America's energy/national security crisis.

Conclusion

If these truths are evident, the recurring question is why do we not do more in the area of biofuels and development of other alternative fuels in the face of *The War-Over-Oil?* We hear more about the problems associated with alternatives to oil—especially ethanol and biofuels—than we do about the problems associated with oil. The public, policy makers, and industry leaders need to reset their moral compasses and accept their responsibility in bring about alternatives to gasoline in the motor fuels market.

Should government or industry pay for these changes? That is easy. The government and industry do not pay for anything—consumers and taxpayers pay for everything. Therefore, consumers should have the right to choose what they buy at the pump. Thirty years of recent history, a war on terrorism in every airport, and troops deployed in our most recent War Over Oil demonstrates that we cannot rely on the free market, or that there is market failure in developing alternatives. We cannot continue to hope that somehow the oil industry will discover a perfect fuel before world crude oil demand doubles in the next twenty years. Freedom is not free and neither is energy security. There is an added social cost to oil, in the form of a negative externality or decrease in our overall security, and thus there should be corollary value to alternative fuels. How do we best cost-share the burden of oil dependence?

The war over oil really comes down to a war over the hearts, minds, and pocketbooks of the driving public. Can we embrace ethanol, second and third generation biofuels, natural gas and electric vehicles and electric plug-ins as we have embraced Starbucks, spring water and supporting our troops? We pay three dollars for a

Is the War Over Oil?

cup of coffee or a liter of spring water. We must remember this is not just a matter of comfort, but of security.

Everyone needs to accept his or her role and become responsible for their own energy/national security. Each of us needs to be morally responsible enough not to pass on or swallow the "alternative-fuel-technology-world-is-flat" bait being fed to consumers to keep them on shore fishing for some perfect fuel that is going to magically appear on their hook. Please do not succumb to the false hope of a perfect fuel; recognize that the countries (not companies) that own 80% of the world's oil are not going to help. Those countries are not going to voluntarily embrace alternative fuels (which most cannot produce) and write off their stranded oil assets. To not move forward with biofuels immediately simply defies logic, as well as the principles of democracy and capitalism.

Just like everything else, our energy policy and progress on energy/national security will come down to an agreement over the value of death and taxes—or the real value of alternative fuels. If the real cost of gasoline in 1990 was about $4.00 (including the indirect cost of protecting the Persian Gulf, oil subsidies, health effects, etc.) and the price of 2nd generation biofuels today is $2.30, what's there to fight about? [1]

Suggested Reading

1. *Winning the Oil Endgame*, by Amory B. Lovins, published by the Rocky Mountain Institute in cooperation with the Department of Defense.

2. *Freedom from Oil*, David Sandalow, published by McGraw Hill.

3. *Blood and Oil: The Dangers and Consequences of America's Growing Dependence on Imported Petroleum*, by Michael Klare, published by Henry Holt and Company (an Owl Book)

4. *Energy Security Challenges for the 21st Century*, by Gal Luft and Anne Korin, published by Praeger Security International.

5. *Beyond Oil: The View from Hubbert's Peak*, by Kenneth S. Deffeyes, published by Hill and Wang (a division of Farrar, Straus and Giroux)

6. *Turning Oil Into Salt: Energy Independence Through Fuel Choice, Anne Korin, Gal Luft, published by* BookSurge Publishing

7. *Energy Victory*, by Robert Zubrin, published by Prometheus Books

8. *Over a Barrel: Breaking the Middle East Oil Cartel*, by Raymond J. Learsy, published by Nelson Current

9. *Twilight in the Desert: The Coming Saudi Oil Shock and the World Economy* by Matthew R. Simmons, published by John Wiley & Sons, Inc.

10. *The End of Oil: On the Edge of a Perilous New World*, by Paul Roberts, published by Houghton Mifflin Company (A Mariner Book).

11. *The Empty Tank: Oil, Gas, Hot Air, and The Coming Global Financial Catastrophe*, by Jeremy Leggett, published by Random House

12. *The Plan: How To Rescue Society When The Oil Stops – Or The Day Before,* by Edwin Black, published by Dialog Press

13. *Crude World: The Violent Twilight of Oil*, by Peter Maass, published by Alfred A. Knoff (Random House)

Endnotes

1. Senator John McCain (R-AZ), McNeil/Lehrer News Hour, 1998

2. Clean Fuels Foundation Energy Security Briefing, December 17, 2009, Sam Ori, Senior Director of Policy, Securing America's Future Energy (SAFE).

3. *Energy Security Challenges for the 21st Century*, by Gal Luft and Anne Korin, published by Praeger Security International.

4. Wall Street Journal, Chip Cummins, Tuesday, December 19, 2006, Page A1

5. Testimony of former CIA Director James Woolsey, Member of the National Energy Commission, before the Senate Finance Committee, April 19, 2007.

6. *Crude World: The Violent Twilight of Oil*, by Peter Maass, published by Alfred A. Knoff (Random House)

7. http://millercenter.org/scripps/archive/speeches/detail/3425

8. *$4 gasoline and 4,000 troops: The Not So -- Hidden Costs of Oil,* Burl Haigwood, Clean Fuels Blog, March 27, 2008.

9. *Converting Cellulose Into Ethanol and Other Biofuels,* Clean Fuels Foundation, October 2009

The Future of Methanol

GREG DOLAN

I n the United States, there are over seven million ethanol flexible fuel vehicles (FFV) on the road, although
the vast majority has never seen a drop of ethanol in
their fuel tanks. FFV technology actually began with
20,000 methanol/gasoline cars sold in the 1980s and
1990s. The Renewable Fuel Standard (RFS) established by the US Congress in
2007, calls for the use of 36
billion gallons of renewable
fuels by 2022, which many
translated into a mandate for
corn ethanol and cellulosic
ethanol. The RFS allows for
any renewable alcohol fuel to
count, including biometha-

Gregory A. Dolan is Vice President for Com-
munications and Policy at the Methanol
Institute. From April 2001 through June
2001, Mr. Dolan served as Deputy Executive
Director of the US Fuel Cell Council. Mr.
Dolan spent a decade as a public relations
officer in New York State government in
Albany, serving in a variety of public information positions for the Departments of Environmental Conservation and Transportation,
and the NYS Energy Research and Development Authority .

nol, which may prove to be the superior alcohol from an energy efficiency and economic basis.

Methanol has a long proud history dating back to ancient times when Egyptians formed methanol as a byproduct of charcoal fabrication from wood, which was then used to preserve mummies. Not much has changed in the intervening centuries to improve the process. In 1923, world methanol production stood at just 30,000 tons (one ton of methanol contains 333 gallons), distilled from three million tons of wood feedstock. That year, Matthias Pier of BASF produced the first railcar load of synthetic methanol from a converted ammonia loop. In post-World War II Germany, methanol was produced from petroleum liquids and coal for fuel use. In the 1960s and 1970s, companies like ICI in the United Kingdom and Germany's Lurgi began developing specialized catalysts for methanol synthesis from natural gas in low-pressure processes. Over the next two decades the methanol industry would grow from a "captive" market with plants located next to their downstream derivative (ie. formaldehyde or acetic acid typically), to a global "merchant" market with methanol widely exported around the world.

In 2008, world methanol demand topped 42 million tons or roughly 14 billion gallons. This volume of consumption is on a par with global ethanol fuel demand. Fully 65% of global methanol consumption is product traded from one region/country to another, making methanol one of the world's most widely distributed chemical commodities. Over the past several years, the face of the global methanol industry has changed dramatically. Referred to in the industry as a "rationalization," plants in regions with rapidly increasing natural gas feedstock costs have been closed as new "mega" methanol plants are built in countries where natural gas is more plentiful and less expensive. These "mega" methanol plants have capacities of 5,000 tons-per-day (600 million gallons per year). While there are just a handful of these mega plants, each one represents close to 5% of global production. Production capacity in North America and Western Europe fell from 13.3 million tons in 1999, to just 4.6 million tons in 2007. During this same time period, production capacity jumped from 13.1 million tons to over 24.5 million tons in South America (led by Trinidad and Tobago) and the Middle East. In 2007, China became the world's largest methanol producer and consumer, with the breakneck pace of new methanol plant construction building further momentum. China's methanol production capacity stood at just 4.4 million metric tons in 2000, and grew to a whopping 28 million metric tons by the end of 2009. Within five to seven years, China's methanol production could soar to 40-50 million metric tons, with the vast majority of this growth based on the gasification of coal and coke oven gas for methanol production.

Outside of China, most of the world's methanol production today comes from the steam reformation of natural gas, characterized by the two-step equation:

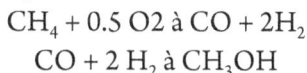

$$CH_4 + 0.5\ O2\ à\ CO + 2H_2$$
$$CO + 2\ H_2\ à\ CH_3OH$$

The methanol production process involves four basic steps (see figure 1): (1) feed gas purification to remove natural gas components like sulphur that can poison catalysts; (2) steam reforming saturating the hydrocarbons to produce a synthesis gas of carbon dioxide and hydrogen; (3) methanol synthesis by passing the syn-

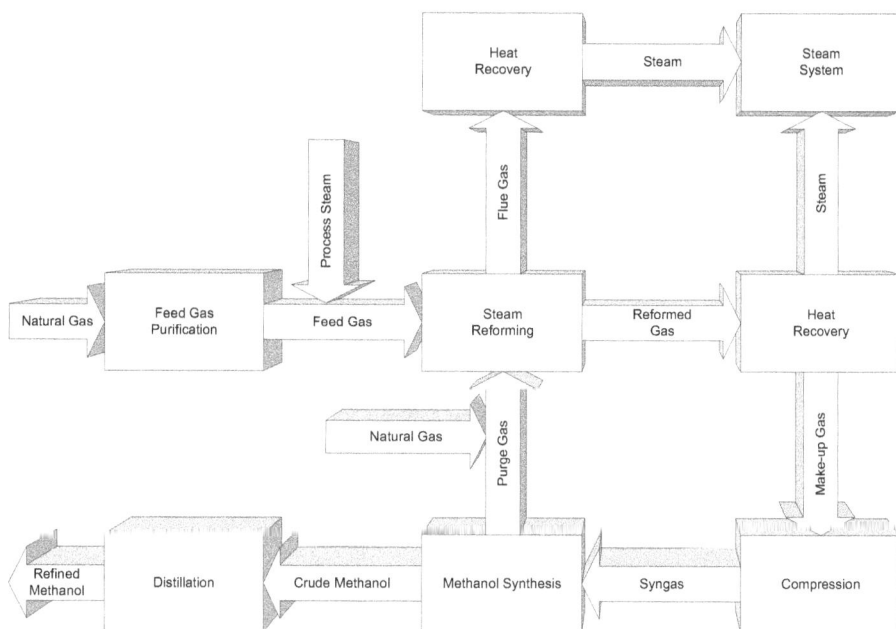

Figure 1. *Conventional Methanol Production*

thesis gas over a catalyst bed at high temperatures and pressures to produce crude liquid methanol; and (4) distillation typically accomplished in a two-step process to remove water and some ethanol created in the process. The finished methanol must meet rigorous purity standards generally on the order of 99.85% (ASTM D-1152/97 and IMPCA Reference Specification January 2008).

When using biomass as a feedstock for biofuel production there are four basic production pathways: (1) biochemical conversion using enzymes and microorganisms to breakdown biomass into sugars used for fuel production; (2) thermochemical conversion employing heat energy and chemical catalysts to convert biomass into fuels; (3) gasification to dissociate biomass in an high-temperature, oxygen-starved environment to produce synthesis gas; and (4) pyrolysis using high temperatures in an oxygen-free environment to encourage the decomposition of biomass. As the simplest alcohol, methanol can be produced from virtually any organic material using some form of these processes. However, the most common methods employed to produce methanol from biomass involve the gasification of "dry biomass" (forest thinnings, waste wood, pulp mill byproducts, municipal solid waste), and the fermentation of "wet" biomass (animal manure, wastewater, industrial wastewater, algae, seaweed) typically through anaerobic digestion.

Biomass gasification for methanol production is especially attractive as high carbon conversion rates and fuel yields mean that the biomass resource can be completely utilized. By comparison, conventional production processes for the biochemical conversion of plant starch and oil plants uses only a small fraction of the biomass feedstock. For example, it is understood that producing ethanol from corn produces 7.2 dry tonnes per hectare per year, or 76 GJ/ha/year. Whereas the production of methanol from wood yields 15 dry tonnes/ha/year, or the equivalent of 177 GJ/ha/year. Put another way, through gasification one ton of woody biomass can produce 165 gallons of methanol, while the hoped for yields for cellulosic ethanol are targeted to around 80-90 gallons of fuel per ton of biomass.

Besides being a most convenient energy storage material and a suitable transportation fuel, methanol can also be catalytically converted to ethylene and/or propylene, the building blocks of synthetic hydrocarbons and their products. Further, ExxonMobil has developed technology to produce high purity gasoline from methanol. Outside of emerging energy fuel markets, methanol is an essential chemical commodity. Methanol is a basic building block for hundreds of chemicals such as formaldehyde and acetic acid used in products ranging from building materials and plastics, to paints, adhesives and solvents.

We are now seeing the emergence of commercial technologies to produce methanol from power plant and manufacturing plant emissions of carbon dioxide, and pilot demonstrations of technologies to catalytically produce methanol from atmospheric CO_2. Japan's Mitsubishi Heavy Industries has signed a license agreement with Bahrain's Gulf Petrochemical Industries Company to recover carbon dioxide from flue gases emitted and existing petrochemical plant for use in methanol production. By 2010, MHI plans to capture 450 metric tons of CO_2 per day, using a proprietary solvent that recovers 90% of the carbon dioxide in the flue gas. In Iceland, Carbon Recycling International is targeting converting CO_2 from emission stacks into the renewable methanol. The company is initially targeting geothermal plants, but expected the approach to be particularly appropriate for the aluminum and ferrosilicon plants of Iceland. The company combines captured and cleaned CO_2 with hydrogen from electrolysis. While in Singapore, researchers at Singapore's Institute of Bioengineering and Nanotechnology have discovered a new process using d N-heterocyclic carbenes (NHCs) as an organocatalyst, then adds hydrosilicane—a combination of silica and hydrogen—and water to make methanol. The process can be completed at room temperatures in the presence of oxygen, unlike previously discovered methods using heavy metal catalysts with toxic and unstable components. The new process also uses much less energy and takes less time than previous methods. Finding a way to capture the billions of tons of carbon dioxide emitted from the world's coal-fired power plants—which make up about half the world's total emissions—and other sources is seen as a critical means of combating global warming.

Biomass Gasification Challenges

The production of methanol from natural gas, coal or biomass share a number of basic processing steps. The feedstock must be gasified by heating in the presence of little or no oxygen to produce a synthesis gas made up of carbon monoxide, hydrogen, carbon dioxide, and water (along with varying other gases). This "syngas" is then catalytically processed into liquid methanol. While much of the "equipment" for gasification involves mature technologies, the immature part of the equation is the first step; the gasification of biomass. Several industrial companies and academic researchers have developed pilot-scale biomass gasifiers, but few have advanced to full commercialization. Unfortunately, the task is not as easy as simply tweaking a GE or Shell coal gasifier to run on a biomass feedstock.

In addition, with an end product of methanol in mind, biomass gasifiers developed for making low- and medium- BTU gas fuels or natural gas substitutes may not be suitable. In general, gasifiers are classified based on the heat transfer mode utilized, the gasification agent, the thermal capacity of the system, and the technical design. Heat is either supplied directly by partially burning or oxidizing the feedstock biomass or indirectly using heat exchangers or other heat carriers. Technical designs are usually based on coal gasifiers and are either entrained-bed (requiring a fine crushed particle fuel), fixed bed (requiring high fuel quality and homogenous feed size) or fluidized bed (allowing more fuel flexibility and more scalability).

The biggest challenge in the gasification of biomass for methanol production is the large excess of carbon in the synthesis gas. A stoichiometric fix either involves adding more hydrogen or removing carbon in the form of carbon dioxide to get to the preferred H_2/CO ratio of >2. Adding hydrogen allows for a near complete conversion of the biomass carbon to methanol. Ideally, excess hydrogen would be sourced in a carbon-neutral basis from the electrolysis of water using hydropower, geothermal, wind power or solar power. Areas of the world rich in both biomass and hydropower may be ideally suited to biomethanol production. Otherwise, the addition of hydrogen requires greater electricity utilization, which increases operating costs. The other option is to use an acid gas separation process to remove CO_2 from the synthesis gas to get the correct balance for methanol production.

Feedstock Diversity

While the use of corn or sugar cane to produce ethanol or the use of soy beans and rapeseed for biodiesel production may offer easy and well-trodden pathways for farmers to expand income opportunities, they may not represent the best land use for producing fuel crops (setting aside the food versus fuel debate). The ideal fuel crops would utilize marginal or multipurpose lands, involve the minimal use of energy inputs (fertilizers), and offer existing or readily established transport options for moving feedstock resources to the fuel production plant. A diverse and plentiful array of biomass resources may prove to be viable for the commercial production of biomethanol through gasification.

Since practically any organic material can be gasified for methanol production, we should first look toward biomass feedstocks that are already available in a central location such as waste wood and sawdust from sawmills or furniture manufacturers; forest thinnings; black liquor from pulp and paper mills; construction and demolition debris or municipal solid waste at landfills (as well as the methane gas produced in landfills); biosolids collected at municipal wastewater treatment plants; and agricultural wastes from farms. The use of marginal lands for purpose-grown biofuel crops like fast-growing hardwoods can provide a centralized resource base of high-quality material. The world's forests represent the largest potential biomass resources, although gathering this resource poses unique challenges. Today, efforts to remove vast amounts of wood (often small-diameter, dead or diseased) to promote healthy forests and reduce the incidence of catastrophic fire are certainly increasing the availability of this resource .

According to a joint DOE/USDA report, forest land and agricultural land, the two largest potential biomass sources, represent over 1.3 billion dry tons per year of biomass potential—enough to produce biofuels meeting more than one-third of the current demand for transportation fuels. Using mature gasification technology, one ton of biomass can be used to produce 165 gallons of methanol. The production of 10 billion gallons of methanol would require 60 million tons of biomass, or less than 5% of the biomass production potential.

There are ample reasons to put these resources to work. Developing markets for trees that are too small for logging can also significantly reduce the costs of forest thinning operations. Utilizing this resource would also help decentralize energy production, with small plants capable of processing 100,000 tons of biomass per year, and large plants fed five million tons per year.

Around the world, there is an active debate on the use of forest resources for biofuel production. It is estimated that 4,000 liters of methanol can be produced from an area of one hectare. By mid-century, one Australian study predicted that the country could completely "decarbonize" its economy through the production of methanol from forest biomass. Plantations of 20-year rotation trees would have to be planted at a rate of 400,000 hectares per year at cost of roughly $2,500 per hectare. In the process, Australia would create 100,000 direct jobs by 2020, and 400,000 new jobs by 2050.

Back in the United States, the State of California alone could harvest 34 million dry tons of biomass each year on a sustainable basis for biofuel production. The orchards and vineyards of the state's Central Valley already collect 2.6 million dry tons of prunings, tree and vine removals, of which one million tons is combusted as a fuel in power plants today. The state's landfills contain one billion tons of waste, which generates 118 billion cubic feet of landfill gas, with current recovery of 79 billion cubic feet. Rather than burning this gas resource as low-BTU fuels for heat or electricity generation, this landfill gas could be utilized for methanol production. The US Environmental Protection Agency estimates that between 800-1000 domestic landfills are currently flaring landfill gas that could be used for methanol production.

Methanol Fuel Blending

In the late 1970s, the California Energy Commission first began testing dedicated methanol fueled vehicles in reaction to oil price shocks and concern over air pollution. Operating vehicles on neat methanol (M-100 or 100% methanol) had its benefits and draw backs. These dedicated vehicles would take advantage of methanol's higher octane content (100 octane for methanol versus 87-94 for gasoline) by using higher compression ratios to increase fuel efficiency and dramatically reduce emissions. There were problems with cold starting vehicle on neat methanol, and concerns with the visibility of methanol flames in bright, sunlight conditions. By the early 1980s, the effort turned to methanol flexible-fuel vehicles (FFVs) capable of running on a blend of up to 85% methanol and 15% gasoline (or M-85) in the same fuel tank. The use of M-85 assisted with cold starting and imparted visibility to methanol flames. The real drive behind FFV technology was to help overcome the problem of limited availability of methanol fueling stations in the early years of the program. The objective was to introduce large numbers of methanol FFVs, build a broad fueling infrastructure network, then transition back to dedicated methanol vehicles.

With encouragement from the state, a series of initiatives led to the demonstration of 18 different models of methanol fueled cars from a dozen automakers. The state also established a methanol fuel reserve, and entered into 10-year leases with gasoline retailers for the establishment of a network of 60 public retail methanol fueling pumps and 45 private fleet-accessible fueling facilities. Over 16,000 methanol FFVs would find a home on California's streets and freeways, along with hundreds of methanol-fueled transit and school buses. At the height of the program in 1993, over 12 million gallons of methanol was used as a transportation fuel in the state. Through these efforts, FFVs were developed as a largely inexpensive "off-the-shelf" technology, and the challenges of dispensing alcohol fuels were solved. In addition, fearing the potential market share loss from growing methanol fuel use, the major oil companies began introducing cleaner "reformulated" gasolines that eroded many of the clean air benefits of using methanol.

Ultimately, only four methanol FFV models moved from prototype demonstration to commercial availability (Ford Taurus 1993 -1998 model years; Chrysler Dodge Spirit/Plymouth Acclaim 1993 -1994 model years; Chrysler Concorde/Intrepid 1994-1995 model years; and the General Motors Lumina 1991-1993 model years). By the mid-1990s, automakers had already abandoned further development work on methanol, turning instead to work on compressed natural gas and battery electrics.

Today, China has picked up the methanol torch, with more 1.3 billion gallons of methanol blended in gasoline (M-15, M-30, M-85, and M-100) in 2009 for use in passenger cars, taxi and bus fleets. For more than a decade, provincial leaders in coal-producing provinces (Xinjiang, Shanxi, Shaanxi, Henan, Inner Mongolia, Beijing Shi, Hebei, Anhui, Guangdong, Sichuan, Guizhou, Liaoning, Heilongjiang and Ningxia) have been developing methanol fuel demonstration programs. These efforts have involved methanol producers, automakers, and academic institutions. In September 2006, eight leaders provided a report to the Chinese President Hu Jintao titled "Suggestion on Promoting Methanol Fuels to Replace Gasoline and Diesel Fuel." President Hu approved this "Suggestion" and directed the powerful National Development and Reform Commission (NDRC) to explore the use of methanol fuels. The NDRC now considers coal-based methanol to be a strategic transportation fuel, and has directed the development of national methanol fuel blending standards.

Those provinces in the "official" trial stage have already adopted their own methanol fuel specification to allow the demonstration of methanol vehicles. In July 2009, methanol sold for roughly RMB$2,500 (US$350) per metric ton, while wholesale gasoline costs nearly three times as much at RMB$7,000 (US$965) per metric ton, which encourages the "unofficial" use of low level methanol fuel blends even in parts of the country that do not have a methanol fuel specification. China's automotive industry is already stepping up to meet this challenge. Chery Automobile, a state-owned enterprise, has completed demonstration work on 20 methanol flexible-fuel vehicles some time ago and is believed to be ready for full-scale production of methanol cars. Shanghai Maple Automobile, a production base for Geely Automobile, one of the country's fastest growing independent automakers is also believed to have the technology for producing methanol cars. The company has already put its Haifeng methanol car into production. Shanghai-based Huapu Automotive, another production base for Geely has built a number of methanol fueled cars. Chang'an has introduced the methanol-fueled BenBen car. Shanghai Automotive Industry Corporation, one of the big 3 automakers in China, has been engaged in the research and development of methanol-fueled cars. With the introduction of national methanol fuel standards, the large international automakers can be expected to follow suit. Ford, for example, is believed to have the technology for methanol cars. In late 2009, Chinese automaker Zhejiang Geely Holdings Group started mass production of a dual-fuel version of its Haifeng sedan. Geely claims the vehicle, equipped with a 1.5 liter, four-cylinder engine, would use 40% less fuel compared to conventional cars. In addition, the City of Shanghai has announced plans to replace pure gasoline with a gasoline-methanol blend for all of its post vehicles.

In December 2007, a delegation of Methanol Institute (MI) members met with the officials responsible for establishing methanol fuel standards in China. The standards work is headed by the Shanghai Internal Combustion Engine Research Institute, which has more than 50 years of engine research and development experience. The methanol standard work is part of China's 863 alternative energy initiative. On December 1st, 2009, China's Methanol-Gasoline Standard (M-85) took effect nationally, following the November 1st initiation of the Vehicle Methanol Fuel Standard. The

Standardization Administration of China is completing work on a national standard for M-15 methanol fuel blends, which the official news agency Xinhua says is expected to be approved in the "near future" (most likely in the first half of 2010). A number of provinces, municipalities and enterprises have already adopted local methanol fuel blending standards, and experts say the unified national standards could promote the wider use of the fuel. Adoption of these national standards is a critical step towards the use of methanol fuels across China. If just 5% of China's cars used M-85 or M-100 fuel and another 15% used M-15, China would displace 14 million tons of gasoline (5 billion gallons) and significantly reduce its dependence on imported oil.

Unfortunately, the automotive industry in the United States is opposing key legislation that would spur the introduction of methanol-fueled cars. The Open Fuel Standard Act (OFS) would require that starting in 2012, 50% of new automobiles, and starting in 2015, 80% of new automobiles, be flexible fuel vehicles or "FFVs," warranted to operate on gasoline, ethanol, and methanol. By establishing this requirement, Congress can break the "chicken versus the egg" syndrome that has stymied alternative fuel vehicle market introduction. With the transformation of the US car fleet to FFVs, the OFS will open new markets for methanol and ethanol fuels.

In June 2009, the House-passed American Clean Energy Security Act included drastically watered down provisions of the OFS by permitting but not mandating that the Department of Transportation require an unspecified minimum proportion of new cars be fuel choice enabling vehicles in an unspecified timeframe. In the late 1980s, legislation was adopted in California to require fuel retailers to add methanol pumps if methanol FFV sales in the state reached 20,000 vehicles. This was a well-meaning attempt to encourage the parallel growth of methanol fueling infrastructure and FFV vehicles, but in reality it led the fuel retailers to encourage automakers to ensure that the fleet of methanol FFVs never reached the 20,000 vehicle "trigger." The House version of the energy bill may encourage a similar situation, in this case with the automakers encouraging the fuel retailers to slow the growth of alcohol fuel pumps.

US Energy Secretary Steven Chu has stated that the cost of upgrading these cars is "about $100 in gaskets and fuel lines," which we believe to be still higher than the actual cost. A review of replacement part costs for FFVs and conventional vehicles shows virtually the same parts for each model, with close to zero incremental cost.

The automakers have complained that passage of the OFS would "divert important limited resources away from the development of other advanced vehicle technologies," a tired argument used in promoting decades-away hydrogen fuel cell vehicles over near-term improvements in fuel economy improvements for today's cars. In early 2009, the CEOs of General Motors, Chrysler, and Ford appeared before Congress and each committed that they would make 50% of their cars FFVs by 2012. Now they want to renege on this commitment to alternative fuels. As New York Congressman Eliot Engel states, "It is a simple and inexpensive modification that should be standards in cars, like seatbelts or airbags."

The use of methanol as a transportation fuel offers a viable means of transitioning from fossil-based fuels to renewable fuels. Liquid secondary energy carriers have a much bigger market potential than gaseous hydrogen (or liquid hydrogen t -253°C). Methanol can be produced from natural gas or coal in the short-term, from biomass in the mid-term, and from captured atmospheric CO_2 and renewably-generated hydrogen in the long-term. The cost to produce methanol from natural gas is around $0.40 per gallon, and even discounting for methanol's lower energy content, an equivalent pump price to gasoline for methanol would be approximately $1.75 per gallon.

Transition to Biomethanol

The commercial introduction of biomethanol fuels has already begun. Range Fuels, Inc., located in Broomfield, Colorado, is a privately held company focused on producing cellulosic ethanol and methanol from biomass that cannot be used for food, is sustainable, and in excess supply. The company is funded by Khosla Ventures, LLC, and has also received financial support for its first commercial cellulosic ethanol plant from the US Department of Energy ("DOE"), the State of Georgia and the community where Range Fuels will locate its first plant.

Range Fuels uses a two-step thermo-chemical process to produce clean renewable power and low carbon biofuels, such as cellulosic ethanol and methanol. In the first step, Range Fuels takes non-food biomass, such as wood, grasses, and agricultural waste, and feeds it into a converter. Then, using heat, pressure, and steam, the feedstock is converted into synthesis gas (syngas), which is purified

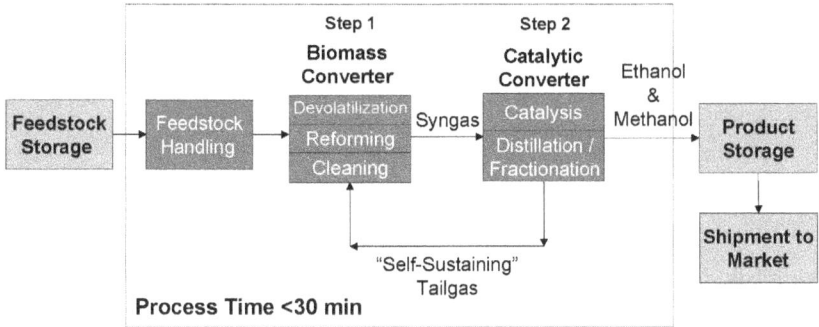

Figure 2. *Range Fuels' Two-Step Thermo-Chemical Conversion Process*

before entering the second step. Excess energy from the first step is recovered and used to generate clean renewable power. In the second step, the purified syngas is passed over a proprietary catalyst and transformed into cellulosic biofuels, such as methanol and ethanol. These cellulosic biofuels are then separated and processed to maximize yield and ensure that they meet industry quality standards. Range Fuels' technology has been tested and proven in bench- and pilot-scale units for over eight years. Over 10,000 hours of testing has been completed on over 30 different non-food feedstocks with varying moisture contents and sizes, including wood waste, olive pits, and more.

Range Fuels' proprietary two-step thermo-chemical process can convert any type of non-food biomass into cellulosic biofuels. This feedstock flexibility reduces reliance upon specialized crops and any single geographic region as a feedstock source, which differentiates the process from traditional starch-based ethanol production and second generation bio-chemical conversion processes, and promotes stable biomass supply and pricing. The process can produce a variety of low carbon biofuels that can be used to displace gasoline or diesel transportation fuels, generate clean renewable energy, or be used as low carbon chemical building blocks. This ability to produce a variety of cellulosic biofuels, as well as produce clean renewable power in the process, reduces exposure to price volatility typically associated with commodity markets. Range Fuels' technology has a zero carbon footprint and very low emissions. This advantage relative to conventional starch-based ethanol production will become increasingly valuable as low carbon fuels standards and climate change legislation is implemented.

Range Fuels' Two-Step Thermo-Chemical Conversion Process

R ange Fuels began operating a first-of-its-kind fully integrated cellulosic biofuels pilot plant at its Development Center in Denver, Colorado in 2008, successfully converting wood from Colorado pine, Georgia pine, and hardwoods into cellulosic biofuels. Range Fuels is currently building its first commercial-scale cellulosic biofuels plant near Soperton, Georgia.

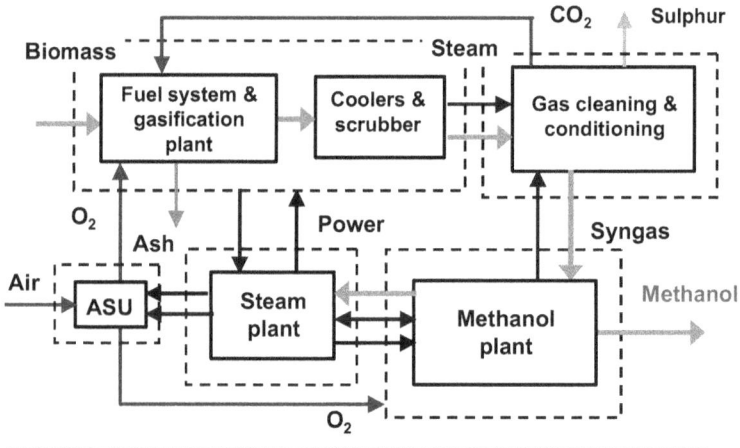

Figure 3. *Block flow diagram of the process configuration for a dedicated biomethanol plant, with balanced power production.*

With facilities in Sweden and the United States, CHEMREC helps pulp and paper mills dramatically increase their cash flow and profitability by enabling them to become Biorefineries. Through the application of their unique black liquor gasification technology, mills can expand to new markets by producing sustainable, low-carbon chemicals and fuels by reusing their black liquor waste for the production of bio-methanol. Black liquor is a biomass feedstock with unique properties. Black liquor is a byproduct of the Kraft process, a technique by which wood is turned to pulp, and is a liquid mix of hemicelluloses, lignin and other inorganic chemicals. Black liquor is already largely available at many existing industrial sites, specifically pulp mills. Chemrec CEO Richard LeBlanc, writing in Biomass Magazine, said that the US has up to 5 billion gallons in potential methanol capacity per year from conversion of black liquor from pulp and paper mills.

By taking the black liquor feedstock, the liquid is converted in a single reaction to synthesis gas, or syngas. Syngas is a valuable building block composed of hydrogen and carbon monoxide, which is essential in the production of synthetic motor fuels and many chemicals. From this syngas CHEMREC has derived a number of fuels and fuel additives, based on methanol. All of these fuels and additives are environmentally friendly and can dramatically reduce greenhouse gas emissions in comparison to gasoline, diesel, ethanol, and even biodiesel.

Black liquor is available at existing industrial sites in large quantities through the normal practice of converting trees into pulp and paper. Pulp mill infrastructure is already geared for black liquor gasification; converting a mill to incorporate black liquor recycling is simple and permits are easy to obtain. By updating a mill to allow for black liquor recovery, a plant can reduce net energy consumption. Another advantage of black liquor is its property as a liquid; this makes it possible to easily feed the substance into a pressurized gasifier. With biomass in solid or pulverized form, this becomes significantly more difficult. The liquid state also makes the black liquor easy to atomize into a fine mist that reacts very fast in the gasifier. Black liquor also excels as a feedstock, with its high levels of sodium and potassium, which act as a catalyst speeding up the gasification process further.

Black liquor also is a desirable feedstock because it is a renewable resource that is not a food source. Unlike ethanol, which comes from corn, black liquor is an available feedstock not in competition with valuable farm products. CHEMREC currently has plants in New Bern, North Carolina and Pitea, Sweden, and is also looking into possible expansion into the state of Georgia.

Based in the Netherlands, BioMCN is the first company to start production of bio-methanol on an industrial scale. BioMCN has operated a pilot plant and recently opened a full commercial-scale plant which is able to produce 200,000 metric tonnes of bio-methanol a year. The commercial plant has the capacity to increase production to an eventual 800,000 tonnes of bio-methanol a year.

Bio-methanol is chemically identical to conventional methanol and meets the quality specifications published by IMPCA (International Methanol Producers and Consumers Association). Like methanol, it can either be used as a chemical feedstock, a clean fuel, or for producing other environmentally friendly fuels, such as biodiesel and dimethyl ether (DME).

Generally, methanol is produced from natural gas, a non-renewable source. However, BioMCN produces bio-methanol from crude glycerin, a renewable byproduct of biodiesel synthesis. From a feedstock mix of methanol and vegetable oils and fats, the compounds biodiesel and glycerin are produced. BioMCN takes that glycerin by-product and converts it into methanol. This glycerin recycling closes the production cycle, because the methanol produced from glycerin can then again be used in the production of biodiesel, substantially increasing its sustainability.

Bio-methanol's biggest advantage is that as a fuel itself, it can be used in automotive engines very similar to those currently on the market, as well as being able to be stored and transported in much the same way that diesel and gasoline are today. In addition, bio-methanol production from crude glycerin dramatically reduces greenhouse gas emissions by reusing the byproduct of biodiesel production. Also, bio-methanol production increases the security of supply through a renewable feedstock, while avoiding negative socio-economic effects, especially those affecting food production and land uses that are associated with other alternative fuels. Bio-methanol can also be used as a chemical building block for a range of future-oriented products, including bio-MTBE, bio-DME, bio-hydrogen, and synthetic biofuels, showing its varied uses for alternative energy applications. Bio-methanol is good for the environment and helps limit global warming by dramatically reducing CO_2 emissions, a 70% reduction in comparison with conventional methanol production technologies.

The European Union's Renewable Energy Directive (RED) includes several fuels which can be made from bio-methanol, including bio-DME. Over the last few years several research projects have been performed to demonstrate the feasibility of DME as a transportation fuel, and both Volvo and Isuzu are demonstrating the use of DME in their trucks and buses. BioMCN has a small pilot methanol plant located in Delfzijl, Holland. BioMCN recently opened its commercial plant in the Netherlands as well.

In his seminal book, *Beyond Oil and Gas: The Methanol Economy*, Nobel Prize Laureate Dr. George Olah states:

> Methanol is a most convenient way in which to store and distribute energy, a suitable fuel in its own right, and a raw material in the production of synthetic hydrocarbons and their related compounds... The ready conversion of methanol to synthetic hydrocarbons and their products will ensure that future generations will have access to the essential products and materials that today form an integral part of our life.

In Dr. Olah's essay outlining a future "Methanol Economy" in which fossil fuels are replaced by methanol, he focuses on CO_2 recycling as the primary source of methanol production. Dr. Olah believes that initially the major source of methanol will be the CO_2-rich flue gases of fossil fuel burning power plants or exhaust from cement and other factories. In the long range, however, once fossil fuel resources are diminished, the low concentration of atmospheric CO_2 itself will be captured and recycled via methanol, thus supplementing nature's own photosynthetic cycle. There are many companies and organizations that believe in the "Methanol Economy," and are striving to make that future a reality. These organizations are located across the globe and are undertaking ground-breaking research and initiating pre-commercial activities for methanol production from CO_2.

Researchers at the University of Maria Curie-Sklodowska (UMCS) in Poland are producing methanol from carbon dioxide (CO_2) emmissions using a form of artificial photosynthesis. In this system, the first step is to dissolve the CO_2 in water. The resulting solution is directed into tubes containing a catalyst that is activated by UV light and causes the dissolved CO_2 to react with water (H_2O) to form methanol (CH_3OH). These synthetic hydrocarbons are no different from conventional methanol, and produce a high octane clean and environmentally friendly fuel.

Scientists at Singapore's Institute of Bioengineering and Nanotechnology (IBN) have succeeded in converting CO_2 to methanol. The IBN researchers report that by using organocatalysts, they activated carbon dioxide in a mild and non-toxic process to produce methanol, a widely used industrial feedstock and clean-burning biofuel. Organocatalysts are stable, conveniently stored, do not contain toxic heavy metals, and can be produced easily without high costs. The scientists made carbon dioxide react by using N-heterocyclic carbons (NHCs), a novel organocatalyst, and then added Hydrosilane, a combination of silica and hydrogen to the NHC-activated carbon dioxide. The product of this reaction is transformed into methanol by adding water through hydrolysis.

California-based technology company Carbon Sciences has developed a process which converts carbon dioxide into fuel by means of a biocatalytic process. Carbon Sciences has created a polymer shell that protects catalysts, allowing them to be reused "up to several million times" and permitting CO_2 to be broken down at room temperature and atmospheric pressure. The technology, which extracts carbon from CO_2, can also be used to extract hydrogen from water. The carbon and hydrogen are then combined to produce methanol, which can be further refined to produce other fuels, like gasoline, butane or jet fuel.

Mitsui Chemicals, INC (MCI) of Japan began operating a pilot plant for synthesizing methanol from CO_2 in late May of 2009. The pilot plant produces approximately 100 tonnes of methanol per year from the CO2 released during ethylene production at the Osaka Works petrochemical complex. In MCI's CSR Report 2008, Masaki Ueyama, from MCI's Energy & Utility Unit Planning and Coordination Division, said MCI estimates that it can convert half of the CO_2 emissions sequestered from its plants into methanol. The process relies on hydrogen obtained from water photolysis and ultra-high activity electrocatalysts consisting of zinc oxide and copper.

Researchers at the US Department of Energy's Brookhaven National Laboratory in New York are trying to mimic photosynthesis. The Brookhaven scientists have successfully used artificial catalysts to absorb solar energy and transfer electrons to carbon dioxide, releasing carbon monoxide (CO). This conversion of carbon dioxide is a crucial step in transforming CO_2 to useful organic compounds such as methanol. These scientists are trying to mimic what plants do when they convert CO_2 and water to carbohydrates and oxygen in the presence of chlorophyll and sunlight. This "artificial photosynthesis" method of producing CO allows for the reintroduction of hydrogen molecules taken from water which produces methanol.

The technology to capture carbon dioxide emissions from chemical and power plants—and even the atmosphere—for methanol production is now moving from the lab to the pilot plant scale, and is expected to reach commercial market introduction quickly. In a carbon constrained world economy, methanol could be the solution. Not only can methanol be used directly as a vehicle fuel, it also can be used to produce gasoline, and important gasoline components such as olefins. [1]